Everything ow
for Su

Everything You Need to Know for Success in Business

— the woman's guide

Jean Harris

THORSONS

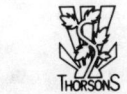

THORSONS PUBLISHING GROUP

First published 1990

Copyright © Jean Harris 1990

All rights reserved. No part of this book may be reproduced or utilized in any form or by any means, electronic or mechanical, including photocopying, recording or by any information storage and retrieval system, without permission in writing from the Publisher.

British Library Cataloguing in Publication Data

Harris, Jean
Everything you need to know
for success in business
1. Business enterprise success
I. Title
650.1

ISBN 0 7225 1957 5

Typeset by Harper Phototypesetters Limited, Northampton, England
Printed in Great Britain by Mackays of Chatham, Kent

1 3 5 7 9 10 8 6 4 2

Contents

Introduction	7
Chapter One What is Success?	11
What can women achieve?	11
Some case studies	11
Chapter Two Self Assessment and Planning	23
Where am I now?	23
How did I get here?	25
Where am I going?	28
Chapter Three You and Your Image	35
Your self image	35
Enjoy your success	40
Communication skills	42
Dressing for success	48
Chapter Four Survival in a Man's World	52
Men and women	52
Stereotyping	56
How men see women	60
Sexism and sensual remarks	61
Sexual discrimination and harassment	66

    Dealing with criticism 68
    Blocks experienced by women in a man's world 71
    What we have to offer 74

Chapter Five   Positive Approaches to Problems at Work 76
    Problems women have 76
    Good communication 77
    Dealing with difficult people 83
    Fighting battles 97
    Handling pressure 99

Chapter Six   Key Skills for Success in Business 105
    Women's key skills 105
    What management skills do you need? 108
    Meetings 124
    Managing paperwork 130
    Making presentations and speaking in public 138
    You do have the skills 143

Chapter Seven   Becoming Powerful 145
    Being assertive 145
    What is power? 152
    Acquiring personal power skills 156

Chapter Eight   Learning the Rules and Playing the Political Game 162
    Networking 162
    You and the hierarchy 164
    Steps to the top 169
    You can do it 172

Appendix — Useful Names and Addresses 175
Index 187

Introduction

More women are in the labour force than ever before — 48.5 per cent of women in Europe between the ages of 14 and 64 are now in paid employment — and Britain has more of its women in paid employment than any other EEC country except Denmark. But the majority still work in a restricted range of jobs, usually the less skilled and less well paid. As well as being found in the lower paid and lower status jobs that are not seen to require much training and development, women also tend to cluster in particular jobs which are seen as 'women's jobs'.

In the United Kingdom women are some 40 per cent of our labour force but only 2 per cent of them are company directors, 2 per cent engineers, 4 per cent Members of Parliament, and 20 per cent managers. In spite of the fact that 1.8 million women have joined the labour market in the last fifteen years, their average gross pay is still only two thirds of that for a man.

However, companies are starting to feel more comfortable about employing women who can do the job and we are at a point where the opportunities are growing. The social trends of the last twenty years mean that women financially support families and take shorter career breaks, often returning to work with more than 20 years' continuous paid employment ahead of them. They are increasingly looking for careers rather than jobs and making this desire known. Men are accepting women at work, not as imperfect men, but as colleagues with something of their own to offer. The number of women making it into the upper echelons of business management has increased tremendously in recent years. According to a survey carried out by the British Institute of Management, 56 per cent of companies surveyed in 1988 had women executives, compared to 49 per cent in 1986.

When children are encouraged at school they will reach the teachers' expectations; the same is true of women workers. If no encouragement to succeed is given it is only the very determined and strong willed who will fight and attain the goal of senior positions in companies. It is well known that in examinations girls do as well as boys in single sex schools where there cannot be any discrimination, and in these schools a higher proportion of girls study the traditionally male subjects such as maths and the sciences. Why is it then that so few women attain senior management positions?

As children women have been conditioned to adapt, not to make waves, to speak when spoken to and to be seen and not heard; and so traditionally women have moved into jobs where these attributes are important. Our upbringing has not encouraged us to move into the larger circles of business and corporate decisions, we have to overcome our original conditioning in order to get to the top. We must learn to focus our energy on a goal.

This book looks at the many facets of successful management, focuses on the particular problems faced by women in management, and gives you guidance on how to tackle the issues you will meet. It looks at these issues and problems in the work context — although the conflicts of home and family versus work are important and major issues, much has been researched and written elsewhere on this subject and so it is not tackled here.

Success is measured by different criteria and success is seen differently by different people; success is what makes *you* happy, and each of us will have our own criteria for success. It is up to you to reconsider, adapt, and develop the ideas here for your own needs.

In researching this book I have drawn on my own experience as well as interviewing a large number of women who are successful, in their terms, in various fields. Some of them are introduced in Chapter One, and it can be seen that all have very different personalities and all took very different routes but there are some common themes which we will go on to explore later in the book.

It is true that a certain amount of luck may be involved in the achievement of success, but if you take the definition of luck from one of our interviewees (Liz Clarke) that 'Luck is where skills and opportunities meet' there is no reason why everyone should not have good luck by learning the skills and taking the opportunities.

Using the book

This book should be *used*, do not just read it and put it on a shelf; read it actively, carry out the exercises, find out the information it suggests and make a plan to integrate the ideas into your working life. Then be prepared to take it out again and read it at different times to refresh your memory and help you put into practice all the things that it talks about. Putting these skills into practice and learning how to master them is the only way for you to improve and grow.

Chapter One

What is Success?

What can women achieve?

We cannot be wonder-women or superhuman in our efforts and be all things to all people. You will not be successful if you are continually being side-tracked into helping others instead of being focused on your goals. But you have to decide what you consider to be 'success' in your life. If you consider being a homemaker and mother to be 'success' then work at that — in that case this book may not be what you require.

Focus on what you really want and need to do, rather than what you 'should' do. Research in the USA predicted that by 1990 29 per cent of women would not be married and this is largely by choice. Only 14 per cent of men are likely not to be married — the trend is similar in the UK. Further research has shown that most women who reach the top are single, either having chosen not to marry or having been married and become divorced or separated. Other research has shown that those who are most happy with their lot or successful are single women or married men. Those who are least happy with their situation are single men. One of the problems with married couples is that there is sometimes a conflict between whose career is most important. This is an issue which you and your partner may have to resolve, but it can be overcome as the case studies show.

Some case studies

Among the ladies whom I interviewed during the research for this book there were a number of common factors which struck me.

In their jobs, their situations and their personalities they were all very different, but they all had certain things in common.

One of these common factors was their ability to learn from their experiences. Not to look on things that happen to them as 'good' or 'bad' but to look at each thing as an *experience* from which they could learn and move on. Part of this was their ability to look positively on things — not to waste time regretting things that had happened or holding grudges against people who had caused them problems, but looking ahead optimistically and moving forward while learning from the past. Many of them actually found it very difficult to remember instances where they had had problems or situations where being a woman had caused them difficulty, and a typical reaction was 'Well, you just deal with it at the time and then move on, don't you?' They certainly didn't store it up for future ammunition! The closest I saw to that was a comment from one interviewee who said 'I really wanted to get my next promotion just to show X that I could do it.'

Another common factor amongst the women I talked to was their professionalism. Their approach to their work was totally professional, and it was not difficult to see why they had succeeded. They had confidence and self-assurance, brought about by experience and expertise in their work, rather than the overconfidence, posturing or rashness of those who are trying to bluff or deceive others.

Liz Clarke

Liz is qualified in psychology and also as a teacher. After a family break she spent fourteen years in retailing, but then reached a point when she realized that she had stopped caring whether a customer bought a product or not. She decided she needed a further challenge and looked for opportunities to move. Through attending a German language class she discovered that teachers of English as a foreign language were needed for a particular group of foreign wives in her town, so she completed a TEFL (Teaching English as a Foreign Language) qualification. At the same time she attended a training course in counselling skills and after a year joined Leeds University as a trainer. The two directors of that unit later set up a private training consultancy and Liz took up the offer to join them, eventually leaving that group to run her own business in 1989.

Although she had an academic qualification Liz did not pursue that area as a career, but had a career break and then began work in a comparatively low level job. But she made moves as she felt the need, each time developing a new facet of her talent and skills, but building on past experiences.

Susie Faux

Susie Faux is a Managing Director of a company called Wardrobe. Her company does not just sell clothes, it dresses business women. Her father and grandfather were tailors but it was while she was working for an employment agency, which serviced mainly advertising agencies, that she realized that women were not getting the jobs they deserved. Part of the root cause, she felt, was the way that these women presented themselves, so Susie decided to open her first shop.

Her aim was a shop where women were not intimidated and where they would be offered a spectrum of clothes with good service and advice as well. She says that women do not consider their own needs enough and she wants to give them back a pride in their appearance. She feels that British women underrate themselves and are consequently too worried about how much they spend on themselves. American and European businesswomen are usually much better turned out than the British, and a comment she received from a European colleague: 'You English look so poor', is very telling. She believes very much that you need to spend money to advance your career, to make you look as though you belong in your job and are successful. Until you look successful who is going to trust you with their business?

Geraldine Bown

Geraldine is the Managing Director of a small but rapidly growing training company which specializes in planning, designing and implementing equal opportunities strategies. They run workshops and produce workshop packs for trainers who are especially interested in training women, as well as self-study packs for women. They are one of the few organizations who can provide good quality training materials for women which are totally self-contained (open learning).

Geraldine left her first career in teaching to have a family, and as her family started to grow up she began working from home as a freelance writer for her husband's training company. When he suggested that she started up on her own her first reaction was 'I can't do that', but with encouragement from her husband she decided to have a go. At first she didn't plan it as a specialist company but as she was developing training materials for large organizations Geraldine gradually became interested in the area of women and their training needs. She has experience of working with women in many large organizations, and training the men they work with too.

Geraldine suggests that assessing skills and strengths is best done in a skills assessment course. She says 'If you ask a woman what she is good at she will dry up after two minutes, but if you ask what she is not good at she will talk for two hours. Therefore asking a woman to undertake a skills inventory can be unproductive. Don't underestimate yourself, you have a great many positive attributes and you must build on these.'

Christina Gearing

Christina has a senior position in the marketing department of the new International Convention Centre due to be opened in Birmingham in 1991. She spends many months of the year abroad taking the message of Birmingham to meeting planners all over the world. She came to this position through seventeen years spent in sales, partly in the retail sector but also in the brewing and distilling industries, then three years selling the National Exhibition Centre in Birmingham.

In the early days Christina moved jobs to get experience but with no planned development. At the age of about 24 or 25 she applied for the job of an Account Manager in her company (a brewing company) and got it. She was one of very few women of that level and soon realized that the company would not expect her to move any higher. She moved to another company and stayed for seven years but again realized that it was unlikely that she would gain promotion or much more responsibility. At the age of 32 she had decided that as a woman she was unlikely to gain senior positions in a company and decided to change jobs for interest rather than promotion. She applied for and got a job selling the National Exhibition Centre as a conference venue. Her boss, a man, was very demanding but appreciative of Christina's talents, and when the NEC was nominated as the management company for the International Convention Centre he applied for the job of sales director and took her with him.

Christina says her boss is ambitious and hardworking, he wants to succeed and therefore wants the best team around him — their age, sex, and ethnic origin doesn't matter. Although he is a hard taskmaster and very demanding he is willing to give credit where it is due and gives opportunities for his staff to develop and grow. Christina feels that this has been important in the opportunities for her to develop her own career and expand her experience and expertise.

While agreeing that her own hard work and enthusiasm have helped her get where she is now she feels that the support and opportunities which can be offered by a good manager are very important. She received very little careers guidance or advice when young and agrees that had she set goals at that time she would probably have moved quicker and more purposefully up the career ladder, although she is very happy in the position she is in now. That is not to say that she will not move on in a few years' time to new and more challenging tasks.

Christina's husband helps at home and *actively* supports her career — reluctant acceptance of her long hours and demanding schedule would not be enough. His understanding and support are very important to her.

Anne Van Der Salm

Anne works as an Administrative Assistant in the training department of an engineering company. On leaving school at sixteen she took a secretarial course for a year. Her first job was with a small company of consulting engineers and then she moved to Aston University in Birmingham where she worked for the next fifteen years. This was followed with four and a half years at a company of occupational psychologists and trainers and then moving into her current position. Anne has always enjoyed the jobs she has done and because of the specialized nature of the organizations has not had any great desires to become a senior executive in them. Her last move was because she felt that she wanted a change and some new challenges.

She has always wanted to do secretarial work and enjoys this very much. The things about her current job which she particularly enjoys are that her current boss has seen her potential to cope with a wider field of work and has given her a variety of new tasks and experiences. He has let her try things she has shown an interest in and so she has been able to develop the job into wider and more interesting areas. She appreciates his willingness to let her try new things and learn new skills and enjoys the variety this gives her.

Anne says, 'As women we need to accept that we are different: trying to be "one of the boys" is not always appreciated by "the boys" and we should build on the different skills and strengths that we have.'

Margaret Hunt

Margaret Hunt is the Managing Director of Warwick Executive Services, an organization which lets out small offices on short-term leases to a variety of businesses.

After leaving school Margaret went into clerical work at a hospital, and enjoyed the office environment. She left to have a family and during that time helped her husband with the administration of his business. After an eight year career break they took on a restaurant which they ran for five years and then Margaret 'retired'. But she soon got bored and started looking for another job. She worked for a charity for three years, then joined a company in the office-letting business. She worked for this company for some time and although she was a director, the other directors did not give her much encouragement. Although she was working hard and running her part of the business well, Margaret did not feel appreciated, so in 1979 she and her husband decided to try and go it alone. This was during the recession and things were difficult at first, but the business gradually took off and they now have six branches. Margaret deals with all the day-to-day running of the organization, including dealings with estate agents and office owners, while her husband deals with the contract work and alterations needed to the office plus helping with the marketing and financial side.

When I asked her about career planning, Margaret agreed that she has set herself goals which she has aimed for. She needs a sense of achievement, this is important to her, but she also wants to enjoy the job. The goals she has set herself tend to have been short-term, i.e. one or two years hence, and seen in terms of achievement rather than a particular job.

One piece of advice she believes is important is 'You should always learn from experience, ask yourself "What did I do wrong?" and then avoid it the next time.'

Anne Dixson

After leaving University, Anne went to Canada with her husband where she worked as a research assistant. She continued this work on returning to the UK and gradually became more involved in the public relations side of her company. Later, her husband's job required a move to another part of the UK, and the only la company in the area which was likely to make use of her PR was British Aerospace. She got a job with them and worked there for some years until another move by her husband meant that Anne had to move again, but this time she was able to stay with the same company. Up to this point she had no career plan and had just taken advantage of opportunities as they arose. She accepted that her career would follow that of her husband.

A major reorganization in the company following privatization required a communications programme for the workforce. Anne moved into this new area and 'grew the job' around her. Having been in an operating area she had a lot of experience and as she is a good communicator she was able to develop this role. Further changes led to this role diminishing but she saw the need for communication within and beyond the company at a higher level so persuaded the Director of Public Affairs to let her take on the publication of a new magazine for this purpose. She is now the editor of the prestigious *Business Review* magazine and in control of its complete production.

Moves in Anne's career have largely been caused by factors outside her control, but each time she has looked for opportunities and used the move as a step up.

Clare Gallagher

Clare studied mechanical engineering at university and joined ICI as a technical support engineer, moved to building services project engineer on another site, and later went to Huddersfield first as plant engineer and then operations manager. The move to Huddersfield involved her husband having to travel further to his job to come with her. She later divorced and remarried. During her time as operations manager she took six months' maternity ~~ and now has an eighteen-month-old daughter.

production planning manager involves planning what
en to make it and the organization of raw
s liaison with other businesses served by
nplex network manufacturing a thousand
which includes thirty plants.
pany having graduate training schemes your

career will not be organized for you,' Clare says. 'You are the master of your own destiny but within the bounds of what is available at the time. You take the opportunities as they come and move into those opportunities which are available.'

Clare knew that she wanted a career and what was important to her was to keep being challenged and stretched; therefore she looked for moves which would give her these opportunities as well as working her way up the ladder. She advises, 'If you set career goals there is a danger of being too specific and too exact and therefore becoming disappointed and disillusioned. The early ambitions of youthful enthusiasm soon become tempered with realism. You need balance and perspective in your job, at the end of the day you should ask yourself the question "What do you *really* want?" i.e. what is most important to you?'

Although women now in their twenties may have been through a university situation where they were genuinely accepted as equals even in the departments where women were unusual, those of the earlier generation who joined departments in universities and colleges where women were not the norm will have encountered the difficulties of being accepted during their university career. Clare tells the story that when she arrived in the engineering group at technical college on the first day her colleagues said, 'I think you've got the wrong floor — we're the engineering course.' Clare told them in no uncertain terms that she was in the right place! Clare has had many such problems as she has worked her way up in her career, and says that she has become used to the problems over the years — problems such as no female toilets in her area of the plant, and whistles and comments by people on the shop floor. She says you need to be resilient and determined, even have a pioneering spirit. She also commented that as she has been promoted to a higher level more people take notice of her and therefore it has built her own confidence as she has gone up the ladder.

Janet Rubin

Janet is the eldest of five children, having one sister and three brothers younger than her. Her early years in education did not bring academic success and Janet did not see herself as a high achiever, but by the time she was sixteen and choosing 'A' Levels at Sixth Form College she had decided that education would be the best route to a 'good job', and was thinking in terms of a career rather than 'just a job of work'. She had role models within her family, her grandmother who had run a small retailing business of her own and who was a driving force in the family and her own mother who worked from when Janet was ten onwards.

At Sixth Form College she was advised by a lecturer not to study for domestic science as one of her 'A' Levels but to keep her options open and to choose more academic subjects. This is advice that she has subsequently been very grateful for. After Sixth Form college she did have a look at a domestic science college but decided that it was not for her and chose to go to university, where she enrolled on a joint honours degree to read economics and economic history. At the end of the second year, however, she changed to a single honours degree in ecomonics: by that time she had decided that she wanted a career in business, something creative and oriented towards people which led her to look at personnel or marketing as her options. These are both highly competitive areas with many people trying to get in, but Janet's clear ideas about her career were very useful, and at university she had specialized in subject options that would prepare her for her chosen route.

Her first job was in personnel with United Biscuits, a company she had already worked for as a student. She spent her first year on the graduate trainee scheme which gave her an opportunity to work in and look at a number of departments around the company; after that she was placed as a personnel officer in one of their offices.

After eighteen months she felt that the job with United Biscuits was not stimulating her enough and so she started job hunting again. She got a job in the personnel department of an insurance company in the City of London. While working at this job she was reporting to a personnel executive who became an important mentor. He supported and encouraged her and gave her the opportunities to develop a broad range of skills which helped her to gain 'professional credibility'.

After six months the company was moving from the City to Surrey. Janet was by now married and living in Hertfordshire but agreed to move with the company (rather to their surprise) but of course expected a relocation allowance. Janet was the first woman the company had moved, they were not used to seeing 'career women' within the organization, therefore they were not prepared to treat her the same as her male colleagues. The relocation package she received included a claw-back clause expecting her to stay for at least two years with the company or pay back the allowance. None of her male colleagues was offered this condition in his relocation package. However, Janet accepted because the move meant promotion and new opportunities for her. Her husband moved with her and commuted into the City from Surrey rather than Hertfordshire. A couple of years later she had a short break of only about twelve weeks when her daughter was born and then continued to work for the company for another two years. At this time she began to feel that she wanted a change and wondered what she could do to continue to develop her skills. She decided to enrol for an MBA (Master of Business Administration) course, but at first the company was not prepared to give her any financial assistance or time off to do it. After a while they saw that she was determined and agreed to give her some time off, although she had to pay her own fees. In addition to improving her work skills Janet found that the MBA course helped her self-confidence.

Again Janet was looking for a career move. She was then a Member of the Institute of Personnel Management (she is now a Fellow) and was on the committee of their Central London Group at that time. One day during a chance conversation with a head hunter she was told that Burtons were looking for someone in Personnel. She was offered the job as the head of Personnel and Training for their 'Principles' Women's Wear division. She spent two very useful years with them being part of a small team that was running the business. Towards the end of the MBA course, Janet was approached by another head hunter, and the result was the job she now has with B & Q. Janet believes that the MBA made her very marketable, there being few people in personnel with this qualification. Janet is the only female member of the board at B & Q and was appointed Director of

Personnel after the position had been empty for two years.

Each of these women has reached her present position by a different route, some more planned than others, but always by taking advantage of any opportunities with which she was presented. Each has attained a position which she enjoys and can develop in her own way. Some may appear more 'senior' than others, but remember that success is what *you* want it to be.

Chapter Two

Self Assessment and Planning

Where am I now?

To make the best use of your attributes and to improve your weaknesses you have to understand yourself. Your understanding of yourself will come from past experiences and your interactions with others.

To help you move on from the point where you are now you will need to look ahead and decide where you are going. If you set off on a magical mystery tour you won't know when you get there so you need to think about your destination and plan your route to enable you to achieve success. We will begin by looking at your starting point — where you are now.

We all spend a lot of our waking hours working or in work-related activities. The following table shows time spent in various activities for two different women. 'A' is a consultant with her own business, she is divorced and has no children and lives in an easy-to-keep apartment. 'B' is a senior manager in a medium-sized company, she is married with two teenage children and lives in a detached house.

In the right-hand column try to fill in approximately how many hours *you* spend on each of the six topics listed. Your activities may not fit exactly into the groups — for example you may have hobbies or do voluntary work sessions which are not listed — but completing the table will give you an idea on how much of your time is spent working. In most cases it will be at least half, if not more, of your waking hours. Given that our job occupies us for such a significant amount of our waking hours it is important that we look

	HOURS SPENT PER WEEK:		
TOPIC	A	B	ME
Family	6	25	
Recreation & Friends	14	8	
Health & Fitness	5	3	
Self (including beauty)	5	1	
Domestic Duties	10	20	
Work (including travel & entertaining)	72	60	
Total Hours	112	117	

at what we are actually doing during those hours and plan for the future development of our careers. It is worthwhile spending some time doing the following exercises to help you define the starting point for your route forward.

Your present job

In spite of suggesting earlier that a 'skills inventory' is best carried out on a course, we are now going to begin the process of looking at what your experiences and then your skills are. You do not have to show it or discuss it with anyone else unless you want to and it is important that you are honest with yourself in compiling this.

Take a clean sheet of paper and down the left-hand side make a list of all the roles you carry out in your present job. You are likely to include such topics as talking to customers, answering the telephone, completing forms, negotiating with colleagues, writing reports, etc. Include all the different tasks that you can think of. If you find this difficult, take your piece of paper with you to work and, at intervals during the day, jot down all the different tasks you have carried out since the last time you added to your list. If you are not in paid employment, carry out the same listing for all the tasks you do around the home or when doing any voluntary work, etc. Think about your list over a period of days and add to it, you will probably be surprised at all the different activities that you manage to perform.

Now rule the rest of the page into three columns, two narrow ones on the right hand side and a wider one in the middle. Head the middle column 'Skills' and look down your list of activities and try to assess which skills you need to carry them out. This is likely to cover such topics as negotiation, listening, problem solving, decision making, communicating, interpersonal skills, planning, and so on. Many different tasks will require similar skills but it is highly likely that you will discover that whatever you do covers a large number of different skill areas.

Before we go on to use this list of skills, let's take a look back at our past experiences.

How did I get here?

Your past jobs

Take another clean sheet of paper and rule it into three columns, one narrow one on the right and the other two about half the remaining width.

Call this new list 'Past Jobs and Experiences'. In the left-hand column of your list think back to when you left school, college, or university, and make a list of all the different jobs or major activities which you have carried out since, including being members of committees, clubs or societies, and leave several lines between each of these. When you think your list is complete go back and look carefully at each of the jobs or activities and in the next column write down the key skills which were necessary to carry them out.

Now go down your list of skills and each time you come across a new skill which you had not used before put an 'N' in the third column next to it. You will probably find that in your early career days most of the skills which you had to use were new to you but as time went on you reused and developed some of those existing skills and added new ones to your list more slowly. Throughout all our lives from the time when we first take notice of what is around us we have new experiences and build on these as we grow and develop. Some of the things we learn we are taught formally through education or training but some are experiences which take place informally: these are not less likely to be useful ways of developing new skills.

As you discovered in the first exercise you spend a lot of your life at work, therefore it is important that work is fulfilling if we are to enjoy the time we spend there. Research has shown that given adequate levels of pay and reasonable working conditions job satisfaction comes very high on people's list of priorities. So let's have a look at our two lists and see which areas of our work we enjoy most, which we are best at, and which we can develop more.

Making the best of it

Although we have not allowed a column for it in our first list, it is worth comparing your lists of past and present activities and seeing which old and new skills you are using in your current job. Then go on to fill in the third column of your present job list by putting a tick next to those activities you like and a cross next to those you dislike. Finally fill in the last column by putting a tick next to those things which you know you are good at, a cross next to those you feel you are bad at and a 'T' next to those where you feel you could improve with some help or training. When you have completed this exercise look at your list again. It is highly likely that you will find that you have ticked things that you are good at which you also enjoy doing. This is no coincidence, it is frequently true that we are good at the things we enjoy because we are prepared to put the effort in to get them right and spend more time doing them. Keep these sheets of paper, we will come back to your skills shortly, but first let us have a look at your work history.

How did I get here?

Using your list of past jobs and activities to help you, try to answer the following questions as honestly as you can.

- At what age did you first start working?
- At what level did you first start work (clerical, graduate, professional, etc.)?
- Why did you first start working (economic necessity, personal enrichment, job satisfaction, etc.)?
- Do you still work for the same reasons? If not what are your present reasons?
- Look at your last two changes of job, what were the reasons for the move? (For example, promotion, salary, being in the right place at the right time, sideways move for experience, etc.)

Your answer to these questions will tell you the key points to look for when you are making decisions about your work. For example, do you have a tendency to move around a lot or do you stay with the same company for a long time? Have changes in job or career been by your choice or have they been forced upon you by circumstances beyond your control? Why do you work? Whatever your reasons, it is important for you to know and understand them, otherwise you cannot make intelligent plans as to how you are going to move on in the future. Try to sum up your work patterns and career in two sentences.

I work because..

I have changed jobs in the past mainly because ....

Having thought about how you have got where you are now, the next question is 'Where do I go from here'?

Where am I going?

What do I want?

As I said before, to enable you to plan your route into the future you need to know where you want to get to, so what is important to you in your working life? Below is a list of some of the common goals that people have for their careers.

- [ ] Job security
- [ ] More money
- [ ] More interesting work
- [ ] More staff to supervise
- [ ] A bigger budget to manage
- [ ]
- [ ]
- [ ]

Look at the list above and see which apply to you, you may wish to add other criteria that are not on that list, but which are important to you.

Goal setting

It is easier to set longer term goals than short-term ones, so begin by setting the goals furthest away, (for example, two years ahead), then move backwards, one year, six months, three months, etc. Do not just *think* about your goals, write them down, and write then down in such a way that they look as if they have already occurred. For example, not 'I want to . . .' but 'I am . . .'

Instead of just thinking 'I wish', think of yourself in the position or situation that you are wanting — if you have visualized it, it becomes more realistic and therefore is likely to be more achievable.

It is no good setting vague and woolly goals, you will not know whether or not you have really achieved them. Be specific and concrete in your goals, set exact targets and details and put in time scales.

Goals do not always have to be much bigger or better than the existing situation, it may be that you can take advantage of what you already have and set a goal to make better use of something that already exists. If you set realistic and achievable goals you will reach them and this will encourage you to move on to bigger and better things.

As well as professional and career goals do not forget the rest of your life. Set yourself some personal goals such as starting a new hobby, travel, personal relationships, home and family, health and education.

Having thought about the goals you wish to achieve in general terms, think about them in more specific terms. For a goal to be achievable it must be realistic and it must be clearly defined. Your ultimate aim may be to be managing director of a company, but, if at this time that looks too far away and so impossible, then you are hardly likely to achieve it. A realistic goal is one which is achievable within a measurable time span and which can be evaluated. For example, 'in six months time I will be supervisor of my section', 'in twelve months time I will have increased my salary to £30,000 per year'. One good way to set goals is to take a step-by-step approach, so try answering the question below.

Where do you think you can move in your organization in:

Six months?
One year?
Two years?

For the first goal on your list work out a step-by-step plan:

1. I will be .... by .... (date)
2. I will be .... by .... (date)
3. I will be .... by .... (date)

Having decided where you want to go let's look at how you might get there.

How do I get there?

There are certain factors which are common to all working situations which are likely to affect your advancement. The main factors are listed below:

— Your boss
— Other workers
— Resources in the company
— New contacts
— People who support you
— You and your own performance

All of these factors inter-relate and link to form a set of circumstances which will impinge on your situation and affect your advancement. Some of these factors are very much within your control, some you may be able to have an effect upon although not entirely control (e.g. you may not be able to control your boss but you can affect your relationship with him or her) and some factors may seem to be entirely beyond your control. Even those that appear beyond your control you can alter by moving within or beyond your company, but first it is worthwhile considering what opportunities are available to you within your current organization. You can start to do this by answering the questions below.

- What opportunities are there available for you within your current job?
- What problems do you foresee?
- How can you overcome these?

For each of the opportunities you list above, make sure you consider *all* the possibilities and set yourself a target date to achieving them. To help you fill in the questions above you may need to consider the following criteria:

- How does your company determine success?
- How many, if any, women are there in management positions in your company?
- Are there any people ahead of you who are or are not likely to move?
- Are there any new opportunities likely to be opening up in your organization?

In addition to looking at the opportunities which may be open you need to look at the skills and abilities which you have, and therefore your ability to fulfil the needs of those positions. Look back at the lists of skills for the jobs you have done in the past and the job you are doing now which you made earlier in this chapter and start a new list of *all* the skills and strengths which you believe you have. It is not always easy to assess your own skills, but at least you can be perfectly honest with yourself! However, it may be worthwhile asking a friend, a member of your family or a colleague at work to help you and to suggest the things which you are good at. It is also worthwhile leaving this list open and, as you read through the rest of the book, adding to it when you come across mentions of skills you may not have thought of but which you realize you have. Head your list 'Skills Inventory'.

Finally in this section on assessing yourself start a list entitled 'Skills I Need'. Divide the page into two columns, on the left hand side write 'Skill' and on the right hand side write 'How and Where'.

You can start the list now by looking back at your goals and opportunities and writing down any skills you think you will need but have not already acquired, but as you go through this book and as you think more about your career development, add to the list. Don't just make a list of *what* you need, it is important also that you find out where and how you can acquire each skill and put a target date for training needs in that particular area. The appendices at the back of the book will give you names of organizations and sources of further information which should help you.

Making a start on promoting your success

Make a list of your accomplishments during the past year.

- What was so good about these?
- Can you build on them?

For example, if you gave a good presentation to your team, should you plan more opportunities to give presentations? If you brought a difficult project in on time, make sure you *tell* your boss and get other projects where you can be visible.

Becoming successful

The difference between successful people and unsuccessful people is that successful people put into practice the things that they learn.

To succeed you must learn to overcome obstacles, and it *is* possible to overcome all obstacles in one way or another. When a problem rears its head there is a tendency to get bound up in it and lose your confidence — it is no good resenting or avoiding obstacles, they must be dealt with. If you do not waste energy on resenting those obstacles or thinking 'it's unfair' then you will have more time and energy for overcoming them. In spite of all the positive things you can do to help yourself and improve your situation, there are certain things which are beyond your control. You have to accept this and realize that at times life *is* unfair. There is no point wasting time moaning about this but put your energies into finding a way around it and solving the problem. Once you accept that sometimes things are unfair then you can and will do something about it.

Successful people are hard workers, smart workers, persistent, people who pay attention and do not over-complicate what it takes to be successful. Having information is part of being successful, but it is not what you know, it is what you do with what you know which is the key. Successful people are activists — they make their own opportunities and they grab others that present themselves.

All business is related to people, whatever company you are in you will have to deal with people at some stage and learning to deal with people is part of being successful. People can be unfair, unreasonable, unhelpful, or down right obstructive, or they can be supportive, friendly, and sensible. At different times the same people can show all these qualities — to be successful you must learn to bring out the best in people.

Every one of us has choices, we do not have to get stuck in a dead end job or put up with a boss we cannot work with. We have the right to do something about it — and we may choose to leave, but that is a choice which we have.

In spite of positive affirmation and successful goal-setting there are going to be times when you do feel down. When this happens use this as a chance to examine yourself and your situation, ask yourself why you feel like you do and what is the problem that has caused it; when you do that you are then in a position to solve the problem and improve how you feel. Until you work out what is causing the problem you are not in a position to solve it. Use each situation as a lesson to learn from and ask yourself 'What can I do to improve this situation or make sure it doesn't happen again?'

Moving on

So far in this chapter you have looked at your career path, you have seen how you have got where you are now and started thinking about where you want to go. You have thought about the skills you have and the skills you may need, but that is only a beginning. The following chapters will describe more of the management skills you need and help you towards acquiring them. During your reading of these chapters you should turn back to the lists you have made and the questions you have answered here and add to these or develop them as necessary. At the end of the final chapter you should have an action plan which should enable you to move forward into the future and further your career success.

Chapter Three

You and Your Image

Image does not only include how you look and how you dress, although these are very important they are only part of your image. Your complete image will be determined by how you behave, your mannerisms and confidence, your attitude to yourself and others, and your whole approach to your role. Not only do you need to have a good image, you also need to *believe* in yourself and let others know you have a good self-image.

Your self image

A good image is one of the most vital ingredients of business success, and one of its most important factors is that you have a good *self* image and let others know that you have. But sometimes your beliefs in yourself are not realistic — they are closer to what you would like to become than what you are. This could cause you problems, seeing yourself as you would like to be may lead you to reject experiences and activities which could be helpful — for example, a woman who sees herself as sophisticated may reject more robust and physically active experiences. This is not necessarily a bad thing, but your view of yourself may become a self-fulfilling prophecy — if you have a good positive view that is fine, but if you have a negative view of yourself you are starting off by giving yourself problems.

What would happen to a woman who saw herself one way (for example cool and sophisticated) but whom others saw as cold and aloof? Her self-image would be threatened, and faced with this her response would be to seek out people who confirmed her own view of herself and therefore gave her positive reinforcement. This would then limit her desire and ability to mix with a number of people and thus limit her experience.

In a working situation you cannot control those you meet and those you work with and you are bound to meet people who give you negative feedback. So first of all you must truly understand yourself and then you can go on to develop a positive self-image.

In Chapter 2 we looked at ways in which you can assess your skills and your strengths, but did not tackle the question of weaknesses. As Geraldine Bown said 'If you ask a woman to list her strengths she will dry up after a couple of minutes, if you ask her to describe her weaknesses she will talk for hours!'

Although we need to know our weaknesses and how we can overcome them, we should not dwell on them; instead, look on them positively as areas for improvement and work towards that improvement in a constructive way. We should not let them become negative feelings about ourselves. If we are honest we all know what our strengths and weaknesses are but rarely admit them openly; being aware of yourself is not enough in itself to grow and develop your attributes. You must accept what you are and what you have, that does not mean being uncritical or complacent, but accepting what you are as your starting point and a foundation to build on. Build on the qualities you are satisfied with and work to change those you are unhappy with. To grow and improve you must be willing to work towards your ideal self on your own. No-one else can do it for you, others can help and support, can teach and advise, but you are the one who must do it. And you *can* do it — you have already made the first steps.

As with your career goals you should be realistic with your personal goals — if you are always trying to be perfect you will have difficulties and you will be disappointed. If you cannot achieve your goals you will not be fulfilled and this could lead to a negative self-concept, so don't try to change everything at once or too quickly. As you read through this chapter plan a step-by-step approach as you did with your career goals in Chapter 2.

You can and should take steps to make things happen, growth is motivated from within you and will enable you to pursue your ideal self on your own. A positive self-image will affect how you respond to events around you, react to others, view others and view life in general. It is vital for your success and well being, and is surprisingly easy to achieve.

Building your self-image is the most important first step to success, but as your self-image grows so will your capability to work better, your achievement will grow and so your self-esteem will grow. Therefore it is not only the first step but it is a self-perpetuating route to continued improvement. When your self-esteem is high you will overcome problems instead of blaming them, you will put yourself forward and achieve more and the better you feel about yourself the better other people will feel about you. You will have new confidence to deal with all aspects of your life and work.

The image you have of yourself has been developed throughout your life by the messages and feedback you have had from parents, friends, and the whole environment around you. Because this process has been going on all through your life, it is quite possible that many of the beliefs that you have about yourself are destructive and it is certain that some of them are out of date. That does not mean that we are stuck and trapped with that self-image, we can and should learn to change and improve it. Changing bad habits may not be easy but you *can* do it and the rewards make it worthwhile.

You are bound to meet people who give you negative feedback and you must not be dismayed by this. Provided you believe in yourself and what you are doing then you are quite capable of achieving any of the goals that you set yourself. We all have untapped resources, the key is believing in ourselves. Women have a tendency to underestimate their achievements and abilities and are held back in their professional growth by fears such as fear of failure, fear of criticism, fear of taking risks, and even fear of winning or being successful. All of these can be overcome if you look positively on each situation, and see each event as an opportunity. For example, overcome fear of failure by looking on each opportunity as a chance to learn, learn even from your mistakes, make sure you don't repeat your mistakes and then move on and forget them. Why are we so worried about criticism? It is only because as women we have a need to be 'liked'. More important than being liked is gaining respect, therefore bear in mind that when somebody criticizes you they are considering you are important enough to take notice of so look upon their criticism as a way of improving yourself — if they didn't think you were worth worrying about they would not bother to say it in the first place.

If you learn to be an optimist and look on the positive side of things, that will improve the value of what you do not only to yourself but also to others. The pessimist says 'I got 50 per cent of the job wrong' but the optimist says 'I got 50 per cent of the job right!' Learn to look on the bright side. You have already looked at your skills and attributes in Chapter One, you have seen that you have carried out a number of roles in your life successfully and you have learned a great deal from each of these experiences. Learning to think positively, believe in yourself and enjoy it is the first and most important step towards your success. Many women have done it before you, the climate is right for you now, so there has not been a better time before for women to move in and move up in organizations.

Improving your self-image

If you do not believe in yourself how can you expect others to believe in you? The way you think of yourself affects the way you respond to events around you. Have you ever had thoughts like 'I can't do that' or 'I look awful'? If you tell yourself things like this you will probably believe them, and they are likely to be a hangover from negative feedback you have received as a child so they will have been with you for a long time. The truth is you *can* look good, do things you want, perform well at work; the first step is to tell yourself that you can.

How would you describe yourself to another person? Take a piece of paper and write down three simple phrases which describe important aspects of your character. Now look at them carefully: have you said things like 'I only work well when somebody is chasing me' or 'I have to write things down or I forget them'? If these are the sorts of things you are saying about yourself then you are giving yourself limitations. Why do you have these negative ideas about yourself? It may be that somebody told you that a long time ago, or even on a more recent occasion when something went wrong and you did not perform as well as you usually do. We are not innately forgetful or slow or whatever, these things are learned behaviour and we can unlearn them. You can perform well, you can achieve in your work and private life, so you must start by telling yourself that. Start by making positive statements to yourself: you could start with simple ones like 'I'm healthy', 'I feel good today', 'I'm happy'. Say these things in the present tense and with meaning and feeling, even say them out loud or write them down. By doing this you are reinforcing the positive things about yourself and your feelings.

Whenever your inner voice says something negative about you or starts to put you down, stop it and try to think of something positive related to the same issue, for example 'I look awful', turns into 'This is a really smart suit and maybe I should do my hair differently to improve my image'. Instead of saying 'I'm terrified about this presentation I have to give', say 'Everyone who is coming really wants to hear what I am going to say and the presentation is going to go down really well'. These are what are called *positive affirmations*, and they must be *positive*. Although they may not be technically true at this moment, telling them to yourself is the first step in making them come true. It is not a fairy story — do not say, 'I wish' but say, 'I am, I do, I will'.

Another important step in improving your self-image is to visualize yourself as you are going to be, actually see yourself in your mind's eye performing as you want. Think about yourself in your new image in great detail, see it as a picture in your mind and go over it, this will reinforce the picture of you as a successful person and help you on the road to achieving it.

Like all objective setting it is important to set realistic and achievable objectives, so when thinking and telling yourself about your new image do it a step at a time and set yourself achievable goals. Each time you succeed in a step that achievement will reinforce your self image and therefore your ability to move on and achieve the next step.

Role models are an important way of helping and encouraging

you. Reading books and articles about successful women, in whatever field, shows us all that even apparently distant goals are achievable. Stories of ordinary people who have done well are particularly useful and encouraging.

Learn to enjoy life, as well as developing aspects of your work and gaining new work skills you should also take time out to enjoy yourself, explore new hobbies, learn to appreciate the arts and share sports and activities with others. This will show you a different side of yourself and show you that you can achieve in other ways. By enjoying yourself this will help to build your self-esteem.

You can enlist the help of other people in developing your new positive self image in a number of ways. Get a friend to help you list the positive things about you; this will encourage you by knowing that somebody else also sees good qualities in you. Talk to a friend about the bad habits that you want to overcome; having told somebody else that you want to do something is an incentive to help you achieve it. Spend time with people who are positive, cheerful and enjoy life. You will find their positive approach and sense of enjoyment is contagious, and will help and support you. It may not be easy to meet new people, particularly when you are busy developing your career, but it is an important aspect of your life. You should read the section on networking in Chapter 8 with this in mind.

Improving your self-image does not necessarily mean that you are or have to be dissatisfied with what you are now, it only means that you want to do, be, or achieve, better.

Enjoy your success

One of the good attributes that many women have is the ability and willingness to work hard, but we seem to think that if we keep our heads down, work hard and 'do a good job' somebody will notice us and we will get promoted. In business the world is not like that. If you want to be noticed you have to tell somebody about yourself and about what you do, and enjoying your successes is part of this.

If you have done something good, tell people about it, you do not have to be bragging to blow your own trumpet. As well as talking to people, send information in memos to your colleagues; write an article for the house journal or a professional magazine in your field; get somebody to interview you about a project you have achieved successfully — do not be afraid to take credit for your ideas, if you do not take the credit somebody else will. Focus on people around you, expand your contacts (again, we will talk later in Chapter 8 about networking) and let people know what you are doing. When you have a good idea do your homework thoroughly, make sure you know what you are talking about, write your ideas down and send them to the appropriate people. It is no good just being good, you have got to be seen being good!

As women we tend to be self-effacing and make light of what we have achieved. Why should we? It is part of the conditioning frequently brought about by our upbringing, but other than that there is no logical reason why we should not accept the credit for what we have achieved.

It is easy to dwell on failures and it is not bad advice to learn from your mistakes, but we should also learn from our successes. When something goes well analyse it. Ask questions such as:

- When and how were the outcomes recognized?
- What were the circumstances under which this project/situation took place?
- How did I behave in this situation?
- How did others behave?
- How did I relate to others?
- What were the measures of success?

By asking these and similar questions you will learn what has made particular projects, situations or activities successful, and build on those for the future.

Another situation which highlights our unwillingness to speak up for ourselves and enjoy our success is when travelling or eating out. Christina Gearing said, 'It is true in the work situation but most noticeable when travelling that women are prepared to put up with a lot more than men will. We are slow to complain because we don't want to cause a fuss, and so frequently do not get the service we deserve or should expect. It is not unrealistic to expect a good standard of service anywhere, but especially when you are paying for it. Pointing out what is wrong firmly, assertively and accurately is something we must learn to do more often.'

What about our mistakes? Because women in senior management positions are unusual we have few role models to work to; we are new in this game and so we are inexperienced and therefore we are likely to make mistakes. The important lesson is don't make the same mistake again, learn from it and go ahead from there. Don't go on about your mistakes — women have a tendency to be self-blaming and self-denigrating, we will blame ourselves before others. Don't waste time on 'blame', it is pointless and unproductive. Accept that something went wrong, find out how and why it happened so you avoid the same problem next time, then move on from there.

Sometimes we run ourselves down inadvertently by acting or speaking in a way that robs us of our credibility. The way you speak as well as what you say are important parts of communication, and the way you communicate tells a lot about you and your self-image to other people. For example frequently as youngsters we are told to avoid the use of the pronoun 'I'. This is something which you now have to unlearn, and something which women are not very good at. Another useful pronoun when appropriately used is the word 'we'. This establishes the concept of a team. Someone who does not believe in herself will use the word 'they', suggesting that it was somebody else's idea, 'I had nothing to do with it' and 'they' made me do it. The over-bearing person uses the pronoun 'you' — almost as if they are accusing the other person of doing something that they could not, would not, or should not have done. This leads us to another very important factor in image-building — communication.

Communication skills

Self belief is important, but even if you do believe in yourself your communication systems may belie this.

A great deal of our lives both within and beyond work is taken up with communication. Sometimes it is in the form of the communications we call 'the media' — radio, television, newspapers, magazines, etc., but also we spend a very high proportion of every day talking, listening, informing, exchanging opinions and so on. Frequently this communication will take place without us being very conscious of what is actually going on: if the communication is good we will benefit and feel happy about it, but if it is not so good we can run into problems. This is particularly important in our working situation where good communication is the key to effective management.

Barriers to communication

We must be aware of the barriers to good communication and work to avoid these. There are five main barriers to verbal communication between people. These are:

1. Information and preparation: if you are not sufficiently prepared for a discussion or do not have all the information you need, this can result in poor communication.

2. Psychological barriers: this includes things like lack of confidence or over-confidence, or feelings of personal inadequacy. It can frequently occur in a working situation where differences in status in the hierarchy, age, or sex can cause problems.

3. The participants: barriers can be created by the personalities or attitudes of participants, for example prejudice, impatience, lack of willingness to listen, and so on.

4. Language: if the language used is not appropriate, communication difficulties will arise — for example, use of technical jargon or dialect words, poor articulation.

5. Physical: some situations make it very difficult to talk because of noise or discomfort. An obvious example is talking on the factory floor, but other physical problems are caused by interruptions or telephone calls. Physical barriers between people like desks and tables are likely to suggest separation and distance in the relationship.

If you can learn to overcome these barriers to good verbal communication, then you are well on the way to improving your communication skills, but look at the following self-presentation factors too.

Voice

The use of your voice is a very important communication skill. Your voice must be powerful — i.e. it is not just what you say but the way that you say it. If your appearance and attitude are authoritative, but when you open your mouth you let yourself down with a quavering thin voice, this can take away your power. Your voice is particularly important when you do a lot of your work over the telephone where your voice will be the first thing a new contact experiences about you.

Your voice is behaviour which is learned, and therefore it can be improved by training. Your voice is the result of the people you have spent time with when you were young. This is why it is often difficult to distinguish between members of a family (such as mother and daughter, sisters, etc.) on the telephone. So if you have learned it in the first place, you can relearn it now. The 'power' of the voice is not directly related to the volume or the speed. In fact some very effective speakers use a low volume when they want to emphasize a particular point. The pitch of the voice is the feature that makes it powerful. A low pitch is more powerful than a high pitch.

Facial expression

Another trait about the way that females talk is that we are overly expressive, especially in situations where we are stressed or worried. There is a saying that 'Men do it, and women talk about it'! Learn to withhold and keep a straight face; being over-expressive is a behaviour typical of people with no authority.

Eye contact

Another authoritative behaviour is the correct use of eye contact. Staring people out is overpowering but avoiding their eyes is weak. When people meet one of the first things they usually do is make eye contact as they approach each other before they shake hands or speak. But interestingly, research has shown that the first person to *break* that eye contact is usually the person of higher status. It is only at the first time of meeting that this works. The person of more junior status maintains the eye contact but the one of more senior status breaks the eye contact, although subtly.

Body language

Your body language is also very important in creating an impression about you. The way you move and stand and sit can tell someone a lot about your self-esteem. It is said that a skilled interviewer can make a judgement about the self-esteem of an interviewee within the first 30 seconds, before they even speak.

Weak behaviour includes taking very small steps, slouching, and looking downwards. The opposite of this is overpowering behaviour where you take over-large gestures, talk in too loud a voice, and your chin is jutting outward in an arrogant manner. This is intimidating and will put other people off approaching you. The authoritative behaviour is, again, the happy medium. Walk purposefully and directly but neither slouching nor over-expansive. If your walk is upright and direct you will look purposeful and confident, the whole impression is smooth and poised. If your carriage is smooth and direct, you will look poised and confident, the old fashioned technique of walking with a book on your head can help you develop this.

Your body is always communicating, even when you are not aware of it. Remember that both when you are talking and when you are listening to someone you need to give them positive signals with your body. Positive signals include:

- Facing the person.
- Leaning towards the person.
- Having an 'open' posture (i.e. not hunched or folded up).
- Being relaxed.
- Having good eye contact.

Mean what you say/say what you mean

The content of verbal communication is also very important. Although it is only a part of what you communicate to somebody it is important that you do say exactly what you mean. We will look at this in more detail in Chapter 5.

Written communication

In a business situation written communication is often a very important part of giving and receiving information. There are a number of ways in which this takes place from brief notes and memos through letters to lengthy reports and articles in specialist journals. Because we have higher verbal acuity, i.e. women have a greater vocabulary, we tend to use more words, often unnecessarily. We also tend to use feminine language, we use more adjectives and descriptors than our male counterparts. Words like beautiful, grand, marvellous, lots of superlatives, adjectives, and modifiers, are female traits. Get rid of these, it will help to simplify your sentences and shorten your communications. There will be more about written communication and paperwork in Chapter 6.

Keys to good communication

There are six keys to good communication skills, they are:

1. **Clarity:** develop a clear and concise style in all your communications on paper, on the telephone, and in person.

2. **Planning:** decide what your objectives are and take the time to plan what you want to communicate properly.

3. **Timing:** time your telephone calls and try to complete them within a certain time span, e.g. three minutes. Set aside a period of the day for making telephone calls and another for writing letters.

4. **Control:** make sure you control any meetings, for example try to meet in the other person's office and then you can decide when it is time to leave; develop techniques to manage interruptions such as setting a time limit, remaining standing, having clock in your office, and use them as appropriate.

5. **Attention:** give your full attention to the other party in your meeting but avoid small talk and get to the point quickly. Use your secretary, assistant or colleague to screen possible interruptions and do not make use of interruptions as an excuse to put off unpleasant tasks.

6. **Key points:** identify the main issues, make a list of your points in a logical order and avoid things that are irrelevant to the discussion.

We will look further at communication skills, including written communication (memos, letters, and reports) as well as handling meetings and dealing with people in Chapters 5 and 6, but if you feel that this is an area with which you need some help there are courses in various aspects of communication skills available. Communication is too important to good business practice and good management to risk doing it badly: if you feel you need further help in this area make a note in your diary now to contact some of the training organizations listed in the appendix of this book and find out what they can offer to help you. Everyone has an innate ability to communicate which is individual to them but the inability to convey your message well can create a barrier between you and your audience which may take time and effort to break down.

Dressing for success

It takes 90 seconds for someone meeting you for the first time to form an impression, and 55 per cent of this first impression is based on how you look, 38 per cent on how you speak and only 7 per cent on what you say. The way we look includes not only what we wear but also how we hold ourselves and how we walk, but it is quite clear that dress is a vital factor in that important first impression, and is likely to continue to affect people's attitude towards you on subsequent meetings. That does not mean that you should give up after your first meeting, thinking that the impression you have created then will stand you in good stead forever. You never know who you may meet or what you might get involved in. And I have a rule that I never treat any working day as 'just a day in the office' or think that I am 'just visiting an old client who knows me well'. I treat every working day and every meeting as an opportunity to show my professionalism, and always think 'I may meet somebody new today and they could be important to me'.

Some research which was conducted on behalf of Susie Faux's company, Wardrobe, has shown that men in business have no trouble relating to women who look as if they 'belong' in management. To do this we may have to do that bit extra, with make-up, hair and hands, as well as clothes, but it is worth it: Susie believes that if you go to an interview looking the part you can command a much higher salary. She also found that men have problems with women who look as if they should be at home or doing the knitting. The attitude that it doesn't matter what you look like as long as you are clever and capable of doing the job does not work. This has been one of the problems of women of the 1960s generation where 'anything went', but younger women are more aware of the need to dress and look the part.

So how should a business woman dress? It is much more important to consider the overall impression that you give than whether or not you are in the latest fashion. When you dress for work have a good look at yourself, what you see is what you are telling other people about you. If what you are seeing gives the impression of a cuddly, friendly, caring person that is how you will be treated. The impression you want to give is one of professionalism. The way you dress will tell a lot of people a lot of things about you. The following are some key pointers.

In most situations you should wear a skirt as opposed to trousers, women in trousers are seen as 'workers' not 'managers'. The hem line should be neither too low nor too high, either extreme could give the impression that you care more about fashion than practicalities. Take particular note of where the skirt ends up when you sit down. Remember you may have to walk around factories or up and down staircases. You will certainly have to get in and out of cars.

Susie Faux advises that if you want to wear trousers, only wear them as part of a suit. Whether or not they are acceptable depends on your business, for example trousers are acceptable in the advertising and marketing industries, but not in other, more conservative companies.

A jacket is your major item of professional dress. Either with a toning skirt or a matching skirt as a suit or even over a dress, a jacket gives you authority. You may choose to take it off when you are sitting working at your desk, but put it on again for meetings and appointments.

The jacket should be classic and tailored. The key words for business dressing are **confident** and **credible**. Investment in quality is also an important factor in dressing authoritatively. It is better to invest £300 in one good suit than in 10 cheap dresses. The quality of your investment will show not only in the cloth and the cut, but in the wear you will get from it and the way it will stay looking smart. Arriving at a meeting looking crumpled does not make a good impression, and if you wear a good quality suit this is less likely to happen. Also, if you have a jacket, you can take it off in the car or the train and hang it up so that when you put it on at the end of your journey it looks fresh and not creased.

The dresses and blouses that you wear should also be of good quality, classic style and well-tailored. Frilly or fussy blouses and dresses give the impression that you too are frilly and fussy and frivolous. They should always have sleeves, preferably long, but shorter sleeves are acceptable, especially in summer.

Colours should also be conservative. Navy is the most powerful colour and other dark colours, grey, tan, burgundy, etc., are also good. Black can be seen as overpowering, but if it is one of 'your' colours and you feel confident in it, it could be good for you. A check jacket can be very smart with a plain dark skirt, but choose carefully. If you like colours you can add some colours to your outfit with accessories, but do not over-do this, remember being conservative is the name of the game. Jewellery can be worn but again should not be over-done — for example long dangling earrings and rows and rows of bright beads are not business-like, neither are dangling bracelets which will get caught up in your computer keyboard.

Make-up should be worn, but again not over-done. Research has shown that if you wear no make-up at all this gives the impression that you do not care about your appearance and so does not give a good impression of your self-esteem.

A good general rule is to adapt to what others are doing. You do not want to be out of step with others in your environment, but neither do you want to follow if all the others are scruffy and show no dress sense. Nowadays 'Power dressing' is seen as a bit old fashioned, but you are probably safe to go for conservative clothes, and then develop from there when you see what the local 'rules' are, and when you feel confident in your position. But remember not to relax into careless or unbusinesslike dress. It is important to keep up a certain standard of dress and be consistent.

Buying clothes

Susie Faux suggests that you should spend as much as you can on one good outfit — if you can't afford a whole outfit buy a jacket. This can be the basis of building your wardrobe. Her experience has shown that if you look successful you are more likely to be successful. If you look affluent that will help to position you as an executive, she says that you should dress for one position above the job you have already got. If your boss or colleagues can 'see you' in a more senior position by the way you dress and present yourself you are more likely to get promoted into that position. She also says 'Women have got to be women, and then they can relax. Don't try to look and be like a man, be feminine but not overtly sexy.' In getting this balance right, consider all aspects of your appearance — for example hem lines, sweaters, the cut of your neck line, the jewellery you wear and the make-up you are wearing.

Go out to shop dressed as you would for work. That will give the sales staff the right impression about what you are trying to achieve and give you a feeling of confidence. When you try clothes on having the right underwear, tights and shoes to go with them will show you what they really look like and help you to avoid buying disasters which 'will look all right with the proper shoes'.

When looking for clothes find a good shop who will help and advise you, not just try to sell you something. If you are not happy, don't buy, a good shop will appreciate your needs and be aware that you are more likely to come back again for help if you are not talked into something that was a disaster the first time you visited the shop.

As well as being well-cut and well-made, clothes must fit well. A £300 jacket will still look like somebody else's cast off if it pulls across the chest because it is too tight or drops at the shoulders because it is too wide.

Footnote — business people need to do a lot of walking, around city streets, to and from car parks, around the office and the factory. Crippling shoes that you can hardly walk in are neither elegant or practical. The smart fashionable shoes with heels are fine, but make sure you can walk comfortably and purposefully in them and keep up with your male colleagues.

Chapter Four

Survival in a Man's World

Men and women

Take a piece of paper and write down:

> *As a woman I must* ....

Then complete the sentence in six different ways as quickly and spontaneously as you can. On another piece of paper write down:

> *If I was a man I could* ....

and complete the sentence in six different ways as quickly and spontaneously as you can.

Now look back at what your wrote. What did you stop yourself doing as a woman? What did you expect yourself to do as a woman? What are the differences you would allow yourself as a man? Why did you do this? There are a number of reasons for your answers: if you did not allow yourself certain things purely because you are a woman, is this realistic or is it only in your own head that you are stopped from doing them?

Generally we women are capable of much more than we achieve and one of the reasons for this is less lack of opportunity than willingness to grab these opportunities when they arise. This could partly be due to peer group pressure, but is more likely to be dependent upon how we see ourselves. Going back to the points that I made in Chapter 2 about self-image 'If you do not believe in yourself, how can you expect others to?'

The image we have of ourselves will be moulded by the experiences we have had, including how others have reacted with and to us. But the most important experiences in shaping our expectations are likely to be those we had in our childhood. Being brought up as girls or boys is the foundation of how we develop from there on.

Being brought up a girl or a boy

The basic model for the relationships that we later develop with others is taken from the structure of the family in which we grew up. The first and most important relationship that any child develops, whether it is a boy or a girl, is with its mother. The way this relationship develops in the early stages is similar for both boys and girls: children love, want and depend on their mothers. This usually continues until they are between four and six. Typically this is when children begin school. At this age a little boy starts to take part in masculine activities and his father's interest in him and attention to him is likely to increase. He is expected to be aggressive, to run and play hard at games, to be independent and to initiate, and for these he is rewarded both by his parents and his peers. Any aggression he has is deflected into useful activities for which he is rewarded so he begins to acquire a sense of confidence in his own ability. Within the company of his peer group girls come to the scene as quieter, weaker and more timid than boys and therefore are regarded as inferior. This is the beginning of the social beliefs and assumptions that might affect his role and sense of identity later on. At this stage even a mother may give a little girl feelings of being second place in the order of things. The little girl is not rewarded for being aggressive or encouraged to play games, be independent or be in initiator, unless she is very lucky. More likely she tries but is criticized by others, told she is a tom-boy and unladylike. In the face of this the average little girl is likely to give up.

These expectations and differences continue throughout school life and on into college or university. Because we tend to use successful past experiences as a predictor of success in the future, it is likely that we will continue to do the things we were rewarded and praised for as children. In particular the encouragement that young boys receive for being aggressive and innovative builds a greater self-confidence when undertaking new tasks. Studies of students in college show that men are more likely than women to expect to do well, and they judge their own performance more favourably than women. Conversely, although their grades were often better than those of their male colleagues, women were less likely to expect to do well.

Research has shown that throughout their upbringing girls conformed much more readily to the demands of authority figures such as parents and teachers. As well as conforming less readily to these demands boys were also preoccupied with striving for dominance within their peer group. It has also been found that boys are more gregarious than girls in terms of the number of peers with whom they interact and in their dependence on the group for a system of values as well as activities.

We need to get rid of the idea that we must be liked all the time in order to be worthwhile. We must realize that accommodating other people's wishes will not always bring rewards or approval and that we need to ask people things, turn people down or inconvenience them sometimes and it is acceptable to do so.

Teamwork

As women we have a greater need to work with and for people we personally like. You cannot expect to like all the people you will work with throughout your working life. The concept of a good team is not synonymous with liking every member of that team. You can do a good day's work without necessarily liking the people you work with. You can learn to appreciate them for their skills and abilities, but you do not have to like them. You can learn to operate within the team and play the game by the rules. Boys learn this very early, particularly through sports. A lot of the language which men use in business is related to this early association with sports (especially American sports): 'Are you in the right ball park?' 'Who's going to run with the ball?' 'Can I take a rain check on that?' etc. A lot of the language also stems from another male dominated society — the military. Maybe when women get to be Chief Executives of all the major corporations we can change the language and inject some feminine expressions into business language!

Team games have a much greater effect than just the language which is used in business. At an early age when men play team games they learn the concept of 'team' and what it means to be a team player, i.e. having a common goal: that common goal being more important than any one of them as individuals. Another thing learned in these team games is that everyone has a specific job to carry out, it has a job title and that job has a job description — something which you must do as your part in the team. They also learn that no matter how one person works as an individual the whole team must pull together to achieve the goal. Star or prima donna behaviour does not usually work; you will only win by pulling together. Women are used to winning or losing alone. Winning or losing as part of a team is an experience which most women will not have had as part of their younger life.

The job you have to do takes precedence over liking the other members of the team — it does not mean that you *cannot* like them, it is just not essential to doing the job. Equally, there are people who you do not think have the abilities a job requires, but you could like them. Do not let this cloud your judgement: you must not let your relationships impact upon the job. You must separate the professional from the personal, while learning to support the others in your team.

Changing attitudes

The changes which are taking place in society now are producing difficulties for our male colleagues. Because women are now changing their roles at home and at work and showing that they did not like the way that things were, they are also showing anger towards their male colleagues who are behaving in the way they were brought up to. This sometimes makes it doubly difficult for men to accept successful women. They have not been taught to interact with women in a way that is not based on sexual roles. They do not want women in business because the games men have been used to playing with women, i.e. sexual ones, are forced to the surface. We may not be very sympathetic, but we do need to understand men's fear of being powerless to enable us to create a more harmonious working relationship.

Although things are changing and many younger women have been brought up in a different atmosphere, many girls today still grow up in an atmosphere where women are seen primarily as wives, mothers, and homemakers rather than people who will spend much of their lives at work. The notions of feminine behaviour patterns which we are already steeped in by the time we are adults are often inappropriate and can cause problems at work. But these problems come to us in a way that seems so natural that it is often difficult to see them, so it is even more difficult to work to overcome them. That is why we need to start by examining ourselves and our needs, establishing our self-image and setting goals for the future.

It is still a basic truth that women have to work harder than men to get to the same level, and we are also more likely to run up against problems of one sort or another far more frequently than our male colleagues. Prejudice may be the cause, but our own ignorance does not help: for example problems can also be caused by not knowing how business works at higher levels, thus creating blind spots. We will go on to look at some of the skills we need to manage well and the knowledge about business at higher levels which we need in Chapters 5 and 6, but first we will look at some of the effects of stereotyping.

Stereotyping

You are likely to find many people who have stereotyped ideas about women, and you are almost certainly likely to come up against prejudice at some time or another, but as one of my interviewees said, 'Yes, there can be prejudices but the opportunities are there, you've just got to fight for them.' Women who want to progress into management are usually judged on norms which are male since most organizations are heavily male oriented. When women do reach a management position they are expected to contribute in a way which is often defined by men and for men. Because women are expected to contribute in a way which is defined by men they are not allowed to use their natural management style and this leads to frustrations. We will look at women's management styles at the end of this chapter.

First, a look at three of the major stereotypes by which women are categorized:

- that we are too emotional
- that we are more interested in our personal lives than in our work
- that we have nothing important to say

These can cause problems and be very damaging, but there are ways to overcome them.

Too emotional?

To avoid being seen as too emotional don't talk of nerves or anxiety but emphasize your reasonable side. Although it is important to keep up your energy and enthusiasm, slow down, don't rush into things but think first. When you are criticized use skills and questions rather than defensive statements.

Sometimes you will be 'put down' by someone who has rather outdated views. Sometimes you feel like offering a sharp retort which will be a put down, but you know that this will not do you any good in the future. One way to handle it is to temper your remark with a laugh, for example 'That's an old fashioned view' is a put down but a laugh will lighten it. Other useful replies can be 'I see things differently' or 'I don't work that way'. Comments are frequently made which are no more than vague generalizations such as 'women with children . . .' and 'the trouble with women is . . .': when faced with such comments we frequently react personally. One thing we must learn to do is not to take all these comments personally and try to defend every one.

One of our female traits which can sometimes cause us problems is our honesty, particularly in emotional matters. Women are generally good at getting in touch with their feelings and expressing them, and although this can be a bonus in personal relationships it can be a handicap at work. Displays of emotion (apart from anger) are regarded with suspicion, and admitting that something is upsetting you or that you have trouble at home may give the impression that you are vulnerable or weak. If you think you are about to face a situation where you may be tempted to be too honest for your own good, stop and think. Play it over in your mind, plan what you will say and how you will say it. That should help you to handle the situation when it arises.

One of the worst things we can do in the male culture is cry. Crying is part of our natural expressiveness and is a good release of emotions, but by men it is seen as weak, and we should not use it either as a tool or a weapon. Crying is not an option for a man and should not be used by a woman. In a situation where control is paramount, crying shows complete loss of control. It will only confuse or embarrass your male colleagues.

However, there are times when you may feel that you cannot control crying and you must learn ways to overcome it. First of all you must programme yourself to accept that crying is not an option. Secondly, if you have a meeting scheduled when you are in a position where you feel particularly vulnerable, it may be better to reschedule that meeting if you can. Thirdly, your escape route is an option. Whatever you do or say to activate your escape route, though, it must be done with certainty.

For example, in a situation where a more senior colleague comes into your office in a bad mood saying they have some things they want to talk to you about, you must persuade them that you have other things which are more important in terms of priority, and that you are still willing to have the meeting, but it needs to be put off. This gives you time to gather your thoughts and calm down before you have to go through that meeting. In another situation, if you are already in a meeting where you feel yourself getting cornered in a position where you may cry, your solution is to get yourself out of that meeting. If you are chairing the meeting you are in a position to call a comfort break, but if you are just a member of the meeting you may have to make an excuse that you have a meeting elsewhere and need to get away immediately. Again, this buys you time to calm down, gather your thoughts and prepare yourself. To carry this off you have to do it firmly and with certainty, and you mustn't use the same excuse too often! You have to learn to be smart, think on your feet and have a lot of self control.

Too interested in your personal life?

To overcome the problem of being seen as more interested in your personal life than work means that you have to persuade people that your work is very important to you. You need to show your commitment by setting goals and achieving them, and demonstrate your ambitions. You need to leave home matters at home, and not bring family problems to work. You may be worried about your daughter's exams or your husband's health, but your colleagues are not. Do not discuss these matters freely at work.

Nothing important to say?

Being seen by your male colleagues as having nothing important to say means that you must ensure that what you do say *is* important and does have impact, so not only what you say is vital but also how you say it. You need to stage your contributions carefully and use the right moment, particularly in meetings or presentations. Read the sections on meetings, report writing and presentations in Chapter 6 to ensure that your contribution is well put. If you have something to say make sure it gets to the right person at the right time, that it is accurate, succinct and to the point.

Christina Gearing said that sometimes as women we have to force ourselves into situations we may not willingly go into, such as giving presentations. Frequently the thought is much worse than the actual experience and because of worrying about it women may back off and take the easy way out, where a man would push himself forward and worry about how he is going to do it afterwards. This is part of our natural reticence to push ourselves forward and 'blow our own trumpets', but it is something that must be overcome if we are to advance ourselves.

How men see women

In some situations male colleagues see a woman as a threat to their positions and therefore would prefer to appoint people below them who are not a threat, who are capable and acceptable but not very good and therefore not challenging to them or a risk to their ego. This is not true in every situation but is frequently the case, therefore women may be denied the opportunities to advance themselves because of the attitudes of their potential managers. This may mean that you have to find ways around this problem and seek opportunities to advance yourself in areas where you will not be seen as a threat or where the manager appreciates good people rather than worries about his own ego. There are also situations where a woman is not seen as so much of a threat as a male colleague. You can take advantage of these.

Geraldine Bown feels that people are sometimes not ready for the truth, and although they may state that they believe in equality, their conditioning leads them to react differently in each situation. For example if a child is taken ill and a woman has to miss work, come in late, or leave early to deal with it, they will receive comments such as 'There, I told you, women are unreliable', but a man who has to leave to deal with such a situation might get a comment such as 'Isn't he good, helping out like that?' This puts women on the defensive and they feel a need to justify their actions. There is no simple answer to dealing with these situations, and although they are best avoided wherever possible you may still have to put the needs of your family first on occasions. If your reliability is questioned you must ensure that not only is the job done well and on time but also that you point that out to the complainers.

Many companies deal with their female employees differently to their male employees in a way that undervalues them. It is not how you are dealt with on a person-to-person basis but things like the job rating and salary that suffer. Women are frequently underpaid for the work that they do. Women also frequently put up with this, for a number of reasons: at the lower levels for fear of losing their jobs; not wanting to 'appear to make a fuss'; because there is not an equivalent job that they can compare with; their boss will not support them. These are general problems which may be very difficult to overcome. If you feel that you are being undervalued a talk with your boss, supported by facts, can be the best first step. It is better to get his or her support at this stage if at all possible. If that does not help talk to a sympathetic member of the personnel department, as senior as you possibly can.

Sexism and sensual remarks

Men and women working together

Between the women I talked to there were different approaches to the situation of men and women working together, but all had in common the desire to get on with their jobs and none felt that it had been a major problem. As Clare Gallagher from ICI said, 'all you know is what you do, not whether or not it is because you are a woman. There are a lot of common skills between men and women managers, and some areas men are better at and some areas women are better at'.

Anne van der Salm does not feel that she has had any particular problems in her role due to the fact that she is a woman. Although she works in an engineering company she is in a traditional female role (secretarial) and her male colleagues do not see her as a threat. The label of 'just a secretary' doesn't bother her, she enjoys the job she has got and has confidence in herself. She says that when she deals with people they realize that she has got more ability than they may at first have credited a secretary with and she is accepted as being a skilful person and an asset to her department. She finds this satisfying.

Janet Rubin pointed out that men often enjoy talking to a woman, whom they tend to view as less of a 'threat' than their male colleagues, and provided you steer and keep the conversation to business it can often be a useful way of keeping in touch with what is going on.

Men and women working together may provide an opportunity for sexist or sensual remarks from men. When I asked Liz how she avoids this she said, 'I don't give out messages that I am available'. Much of this comes down to experience and confidence but it is also an ability to be assertive. Liz advises anybody who feels timid or reticent to go on an assertiveness course. On overhearing a discussion between two female subordinates about a male client of hers, Geraldine Bown was surprised to discover that he had a reputation for being a womanizer. When she commented to the speakers that she was surprised to hear this they said to her, 'Ah well, he wouldn't be like that with you because you give off an aura'. That 'aura' is the businesslike air of a professional person intent on doing a job, and is one which we can all cultivate.

But in spite of all efforts to avoid getting into difficult situations you may experience unwanted attention or sensual remarks on occasions. It is how you respond to any remarks made by male colleagues, especially the first time, which establishes a pattern. You need to be assertive but not aggressive. If you react frostily to a slightly risqué comment you may get accused of being unable to take a joke, but if you react with a positive and professional comment such as, 'I don't think it would be productive if we continued along that line' this can usually bring the conversation back on track.

When a male colleague makes a remark which is sexist or makes a sexual approach, one understandable tactic (but not the best) is to ignore it or make a joke. Ignoring it doesn't always work, it may encourage him to try again. It is best dealt with on the spot if at all possible. One of the reasons for such remarks and problems arising is because men are not used to coping with women as equals in a work situation, although this is less true of younger men than of men of older generations.

Sometimes flippant or so-called funny comments are made by men, particularly in a group situation and if you react badly to these you are accused of being neurotic or 'can't take a joke'. Again you must not react personally to these but must deal with them in a professional and straightforward manner with a remark such as 'I don't believe that is going to help us solve this particular problem at the moment'.

Many of the comments which are made by men to women in business are subconscious and not intended to be sexist. If you are away on a course or a meeting for a couple of days a comment such as 'How is your husband going to manage while you are away?' would not be directed at a male colleague. Such comments are not intended to hurt but they are very damaging and although the speaker may be meaning to be protective he needs educating. It is sometimes easier to deal with someone who is really meaning to be difficult than someone who 'doesn't mean it'. The best reaction is not to be aggressive but to make an observation on the behaviour.

Geraldine Bown suggested that a good answer to the generalizations which are made about women by men is to reply with a question, for example 'Do you mean me personally or is that a general observation?', or 'Is it a problem for you having women in your team?' There is usually an issue underneath such remarks so don't defend yourself but try to find out what is the underlying cause. Don't make excuses, reflect for a moment and you may find that your male colleagues are less likely to make such antagonistic remarks if you do not rise to the bait.

One of the most important techniques for dealing with problems with male colleagues is confidence and professionalism. If you know your topic, are confident in what you are saying or doing and can hold your own in discussions and meetings you are less likely to be approached in this way or have such remarks made to you.

When dealing with male colleagues who may wish to make your life difficult it is important that you are very good at what you are doing. Male colleagues are less forgiving of women and so you have to build their respect more so than other men. Don't let them catch you doing something wrong if you can possibly help it, but give as good as you get in discussions and meetings. You must build your relationship from a good foundation of knowing what you are talking about and being good at your job.

Many women manage to go through their working lives without experiencing any sexual harassment or aggression, others brush it off so easily they don't seem to notice it even when it does occur. But what do you do when a colleague, particularly a more senior colleague or even your boss, makes a pass at you? Chances are they will start with minor advances to test the ground, changing the subject from work and on to more personal remarks for example. The first thing you could do is to totally ignore these; if this doesn't work, the next step is to keep bringing the conversation back to the project or point in hand. It may take a number of attempts, but it is worth keeping at it.

When you are caught off guard by a blatantly sexist remark, whether intentional or otherwise, it is sometimes difficult to think of the right answer there and then. Being caught off guard like this sometimes leads you to react or reply in a way which might encourage the questioner to pursue his line to see you feeling awkward or getting defensive. Some women I spoke to said they are actually quite rude sometimes when personal sexist remarks are made, but the problem with this is that it may destroy a relationship totally. Others have said that they have a standard set of amusing phrases which are 'put downs' but said with a smile in such a way that the questioner realizes it is no use pursuing that line but does not himself feel so embarrassed that the relationship is destroyed.

Sometimes men that Margaret Hunt meets in her line of business will try to show that they are powerful. Her reaction to this is that she is not overawed but responds in a business-like manner, keeps to the point and shows that she knows what she is talking about. She feels that once you have made a good job of selling your services then clients and colleagues will react well whether they are male or female. She believes that because of her experience of life as well as business, she can lock into the needs of a client or supplier when she is talking to them: this is a degree of professionalism which is respected by those she meets. This is a skill we must all learn.

Sexual harassment is usually most likely between peers or when the female is subordinate to the male. But less expected are the forms of sexism which may arise from men working for women and women working together.

Men working for women

It is quite frequent that men who are asked if they are prepared to work for a woman boss say they don't want to do it. Of men who do work for a woman, some may not sing the praises of their boss in public, but privately will admit that the woman is a good manager; some may grudgingly accept that a woman boss is good at her job although her style is different to men in that role.

There are some men who find it difficult, if not impossible, to work for a woman. I raised this question with some of the women I interviewed and one forthright and honest answer I got is 'It's their problem, if they can't cope with it, they have to go!' Not many women would be this decisive and honest, and would spend time worrying about the problem, caring for the man with the problem and trying to solve it for him. If he has particular attributes which you need on your team, it might be worthwhile and you don't want to get a reputation for getting rid of people who do not agree with you. However, if the individual really does not want to work for a woman, he is not giving her his best and is not contributing what he should to the team. Time and effort spent trying to patch up an impossible relationship will not pay back enough to make it worthwhile and you may have to let him go. This does not have to be done in an aggressive, damaging way, however, and eventually it is likely to be to your mutual benefit.

Women working for women

Sometimes women working for women is a more difficult situation than working for men.

There are two possible approaches of women managers to their female subordinates. One is that most women managers are a little unusual in their roles and usually enjoy being the 'rare woman' and succeeding; therefore subconsciously they want to be a bit exclusive and so may be less happy to see female subordinates shine. This is unusual but may be something which a woman might come across in working for another woman.

More usually women managers drive their female subordinates hard, wishing them to succeed. Research suggests that women bosses are tougher on their female subordinates than they are on their male subordinates. This may be a reaction against not wishing to appear to give favours to other women, it may also be because they want to drive their female subordinates on to become 'the best' and therefore are hard task masters.

Almost all Margaret Hunt's employees are women and she does not find this a problem. She enjoys bringing bright youngsters into the company and giving them opportunities to grow and develop. But this is in the knowledge that she owns the company and they are not putting her position at risk. In her previous job she realized that younger women could be a potential threat but rather than antagonism this brought out in her a determination to do even better and keep ahead.

Always try to support other women in your team and those women above you, but not to the detriment of other colleagues.

Sexual discrimination and harassment

The passing of the Sex Discrimination Act in 1976 means that it is now illegal for a woman to be treated less favourably than a man would be in the same circumstances. But it is in fact quite difficult to enforce this law. Another problem that has been brought about by the Act is that previously men admitted to being prejudiced, but now they hide the fact and it is far more difficult to deal with. However, the Act does give women the right to take legal action over sexual harassment and sex discrimination. But this can be a considerable ordeal for women. Cases can attract unwelcome publicity and although an Industrial Tribunal can protect employers by ordering a private hearing if the evidence given in public is likely to injure their interest substantially, it cannot do the same for a complainant. However, cases are often resolved without having to go to Tribunal or Court: in 1987 over a thousand individual cases were settled in this way, and 33 preliminary investigations resulted in voluntary change.

The threat of legal action can be a persuasive lever.

In simple terms sexual harassment is anything a person finds upsetting, offensive or embarrassing sexually, ranging from repeated 'jokes' to sexual assault. Recent legal decisions have placed a clear duty with employers to ensure that workers are not harassed. But only a very small percentage of work places, probably less than 20 per cent, are covered by any special procedural agreement for tackling the problem.

Not only do the women who are targets of sexual harassment suffer distress but the cost of harassment can also be counted in company terms. Job performance, absenteeism, staff turnover, and morale are all affected. The enormous waste of resources which is caused by sexual harassment should not be ignored by employers. Under the Sex Discrimination Act (1975) and the Employment Protection (Consolidation) Act (1978) employers have legal obligations towards women who are harassed. A woman who leaves her job because of sexual harassment may be able to claim unfair or constructive dismissal and compensation at an Industrial Tribunal. But frequently things do not need to go that far and there is evidence to show that the situation is improving in certain respects: an increasing number of employers are taking the issue seriously and are establishing complaints procedures.

In spite of this, it is best to avoid problems at the start. Acting and dressing professionally as we described in Chapter 3 can help. For example one lady I interviewed is a tall and purposeful looking lady although very attractive. She treats others as her equal and gives an air of professionalism, so even when walking around the shop floor of the factory (a notoriously difficult area) her air of confidence and willingness to talk to people rather than scuttle past with her head down surprises her male colleagues and encourages them to react in an equally professional manner. Deal promptly with any unwanted remarks that do arise. The three key techniques are:

- Use humour, but not sarcasm.

- Discuss the remarks and reach agreement.

- Ask the individual concerned to change his behaviour. Ignoring it is *not* a good option!

If you do have a more serious problem which these techniques do not solve, go to your boss and discuss it in a professional and straightforward manner. Most harassment goes unreported and this only exacerbates the situation. You may feel embarrassed and afraid that you will not be taken seriously but for your own as well as for other people's sakes it is worth dealing with the matter. You may need to remind your boss that employers also pay a high price for harassment. A high turnover of staff means a low return on investment in staff training. It is in an employer's interest to ensure that valuable staff do not lose out on promotion prospects or perform badly in their jobs because of harassment at work. If you are being harassed chances are that the culprit will also turn his attentions to others. It is important that in this meeting with your boss to discuss your complaint you are not emotional or upset. Plan the meeting properly, take notes with you to help if you wish, state the facts clearly and ask for a solution. If you can offer a sensible solution yourself this may be helpful but do not offer or accept one that appears to put you in the wrong or lesser position (for example moving you off a project which is a good career position because another member of the team causes you a problem).

If the problem you are having has been caused by your boss, (and there is evidence to show that in up to 25 per cent of all cases the harasser is the immediate supervisor of the victim) then go to your personnel department for advice or to another female member of management. It is worth remembering that the company is more likely to be able to respond informally before the stage where a formal complaint is made. A quiet word with the man concerned and keeping a close eye on the situation may be all that is needed.

Dealing with criticism

Think of an occasion when you have been criticized recently and try to answer the following questions in relation to that occasion.

- What was it about?
- Who was it given by?
- How was it given?
- What was the outcome?
- Did you think it unfair?
- How did you react?

Answer these questions as honestly as you can and then bear them in mind while you read the following paragraphs. As women we tend to be very defensive when criticized, the usual reaction is to offer an excuse. Do not always assume that a critic wants to put you down, sometimes criticism can be constructive. If you see that someone is criticizing you to get you to improve your performance, then do not reject it. If the critic is a good manager or colleague they will follow with suggestions on how you can improve. A comment like, 'This report is awful' may not be very helpful, but is not necessarily unkindly meant. If you reply, 'So what!' or 'That's my problem not yours' you will never find out why the report is awful, if it truly is. Careful questioning in a straightforward manner, not weak or over submissive, can lead the critic to help you improve. 'What would you like to see done to improve it?' could lead to a helpful and constructive discussion.

But sometimes criticism is less helpful, and women are often reluctant to offer new ideas or try new approaches for fear of criticism. If you learn techniques for dealing with unwarranted criticism you will be more likely to be innovative.

Firstly, avoid your natural reaction to resist the criticism and look for ways to find agreement with the critic — this can be very disarming for them. Try to look at the criticism from the other person's point of view and agree that it is valid for that person. This might be difficult at first since you are used to defending, attacking or arguing when criticized; however, when you find agreement you do not add 'fuel to the fire'. If you find a point of agreement the conversation will then frequently develop in a positive manner. Useful phrases are:

'It is possible that . . .'
'You might be right.'
'I agree with . . . where you say . . .'

A second technique to deal with criticism is to restate what the critic has said but summarizing or paraphrasing what you have heard. Gibes are often used by a critic to give weight to a flimsy comment and by paraphrasing you can control the direction of the response because you can restate the part that you feel is the main reason for concern and ignore the gibes. By giving back to the critic what you believe he or she has said it may make their argument seem different to them, enable them to explain why they think or feel like that or even show that the criticism is not valid. Some useful phrases are:

'Then if I heard you right, you . . .'
'So you feel that . . .'
'So what I hear you asking is . . .'

The third technique for dealing with unwarranted criticism is to clarify the criticism which is being made. This can actively prompt further criticism. If the criticism is manipulative, then inquiring about it will eventually exhaust it: if the criticism is constructive and valid then inquiring about it will give you more information, help you to clarify it, and enable you to correct the problem. Some useful phrases are:

'What makes you feel like that?'
'What in particular is it about this memo that does not sound right?'
'What makes you say . . .?'

Having read this far in the book you will have thought about your self-image, set yourself some goals, and considered why you behave in certain ways. Bearing what you have learnt in mind answer the following three questions:

- Thinking back to the occasion when you were criticized which you considered at the beginning of this section, would you react differently now?
- If so, how would you react?
- What do you think would be the outcome now?

If you would not react differently now then it is possible that you dealt with the criticism well at that time, but if you did not feel that you dealt with it well and you could not react differently now then re-read this section again before you move on. Another tool which will help you to be more positive and deal with criticism is assertiveness. We will look at this in more detail later in Chapter 7.

Blocks experienced by women in a man's world

Old boys' networks

One of the most important ways of getting and keeping in touch is by networking. We will look at how women can network in Chapter 8, but while we are looking at the problems of surviving in a man's world we need to be aware of the networks which our male colleagues have. Because of the way that boys are brought up and worked together in school they develop relationships with other boys which are often long-standing and will exclude girls.

These links may surface again in later life during a man's career, and people whom he has known earlier can be very useful to him in helping him up the career ladder. Because these early networks have excluded women, the later networks will as well. And because of men's reluctance to accept women into their circle it will not be easy to change this even as more and more women are working with them. This is exacerbated by the fact that much of the networking goes on in places where women are excluded, in the men's toilets, during sporting activities, and over a pint after work. Our segregated education system may start this process but it is supported by the continued survival of men's clubs where there is often great resistance to admitting women.

Moving with the job

Sometimes a company offers a promotion which will require a move. Traditionally it has been the man's career which has taken precedence and the wife has given up her job and moved along with the husband. This is one of the reasons why single women have been the ones to do the advancing.

In many organizations where a move is part of a promotion married women are not even asked or given the option to make that decision. Promotion opportunities in large organizations often mean moving locations. If you are married others in the company assume you cannot move: this is assumption without consultation. This may be partly because the corporations are not willing to accept the guilt of splitting up the family unit! Therefore if you are a woman who wishes to advance her career and are willing to move you must make that quite clear to your boss and (if necessary) to other people.

Clare Gallagher tells the story of a chance meeting on the stairs with somebody who knew of a job opportunity going in another plant but who had assumed she would not be interested because she was married. Having made it clear that she was interested and was able to move she then got the opportunity to apply for the post.

The need to move with your husband's job can sometimes be turned to your advantage, for example Anne Dixson used each opportunity of a move to develop a new aspect of her career. But there is no reason why it should not be the women who initiate moves, as Clare Gallagher showed, and sometimes it may mean a compromise of moving to live somewhere in between your two locations as in the case of Janet Rubin.

Threatening the male ego

Some women who are successful manage not to threaten, but many women achievers appear to pose a threat to their male colleagues. Once a man has experienced this he is more likely to be resistant to other women he meets professionally. Women who threaten give the feeling that they are superior to their male colleagues: you may know you are — but showing it is not a good tactic. Believing and acting as an equal is the best way, but on occasions you may even have to hide your intellect. Shrewd young men do it — upstaging the boss is not a good tactic in anyone's eyes. If you know you have the skills there is a time and a place to show them.

Conflicts of values

Traditionally in family life women have had a support role, they have been more concerned with the wants and needs of others and their emotional reactions have been an important part of this role. As a result of this women tend to make moral judgments about work place practices based on the values which we use when dealing with family and friends. The bottom line in business is making a profit and along with that goes the need for power and growth. To show that we are shocked at the way that businesses operate won't be any help to us. This attitude is naïve and it is much more likely to cut us off from sources of information: people will stop telling us things they think might upset us. To overcome this we need to learn to adopt a non-judgmental approach. You need to remind yourself that your main business is to keep your company in profit, that is often the best way to keep people happy and handing out money to apparently needy colleagues is not going to help them if the business goes bust.

Women are less concerned about the trappings or rank than men. In some situations, for example, for the only woman in an all male team, this could be a problem as the woman may accept less in terms of administrative help and support than her male colleagues and therefore be seen by others as less important. However, in a female team the idea of sharing can be an advantage and work well. Do not accept less than your colleagues, but assess each situation and make the best use of the resources available on a fair basis.

What we have to offer

Having discussed the many problems facing women managers and aspiring managers, we must not leave this chapter with the idea that it is all problems and battles. There is a great deal of opportunity for women in business and industry at present and there will be more in the future. Many of our skills are being seen as more valuable.

Until recently women were knocking on the door of a man's world asking to be let in and to be let in they had to prove that they could do it. The first senior women had to be more like men than men. But things are changing. The values that women are bringing into the workplace are the values that industries are supporting today. It is true that there are general differences of approach between men and women and they can each gain from the other. Men tend to be far more competitive than women, more interested in winning than in doing the best job possible, more interested in office politics, more career conscious, and far more willing to boss people about. The perceived view is that women in general are more interested in doing a good job than in career advancement, more interested in the health and welfare of their employees, more concerned to get agreement at meetings and more concerned to give back to the community as well as taking out. It is these very human skills that women managers need to take British industry into the 21st century.

Going back to my earlier comment about support, men are very territorial but women less so and it is noticeable that women do not have the rivalry that men have, frequently helping each other and their subordinates. This is part of our natural caring attitude and concern for others and used sensibly can be to our advantage. Our ability to understand people, for example our bosses' moods, better than our male colleagues can put us in a position of strength.

In our families and homes women are socialized to manage people and relationships and now they are able to take these skills from the home into the workplace. Studies have shown that women tend to be more participatory in their management style and they are seen by both male and female subordinates to be much more caring than male counterparts. Another aspect of women's style which is now becoming more valued is the way we think. People who can be enterprising and individualistic and challenge old ideas were discouraged in large organizations and had to go off and set up on their own. Now, organizations need such enterprising people, and women fit the bill for this kind of creativity. Obviously both men and women use both sides of the brain but research has shown that women are tremendous right-brain thinkers (that's the creative side of the brain), while men use the left side more, that's the part that analyses and uses logic. Research has also shown that women have more ideas transferring from one side of the brain to the other so women are clearly more flexible than men. The needs of a rapidly changing world are demanding this flexibility, flair, and enterprise and women are there to fit the bill.

Janet Rubin commented 'Women are often better at relating to people than men; women have a different perspective to business problems, they are frequently more creative and may come up with ideas that men would not think of.'

It is likely that in the future management is going to get looser and more co-operative — this will make it easier for women to fit in. The opportunities are there, so work at developing your skills, at overcoming the problems, and make sure you get your share of what is coming.

Chapter Five

Positive Approaches to Problems at Work

Problems women have

Having looked at the problems you are likely to encounter in your working situations, we will now look in more detail at how you can deal with some of these problems.

As women we come to the world of work with a number of blocks:

- the desire for perfection
- the need to be noticed
- the need to be liked
- the willingness to take on too much, and inability to say no
- the reluctance to ask for help because we believe this shows vulnerability
- the tendency to work as individuals rather than in teams.

We have to unlearn these blocked behaviours before we can move on to build on our skills. All these blocks are to do with our relationships with people.

Sometimes the problems in companies are caused by problem people — individuals, not a 'whole company' attitude. The male chauvinist attitude of some people could get you down. Clare Gallagher said that the best way to deal with this is to carry out your job in a professional way, so you are accepted as just another 'project manager, or whatever, not male or female; by managing fairly and sensibly you will become accepted. It doesn't mean that it is easy.'

Whether or not you are in a job which is supposed to be 'people oriented' you are going to have to deal with people and the systems imposed by people — as well as being allies and friends people can also be your biggest problem. It is essential that you learn to develop rapport with colleagues and clients and there is nothing wrong with using your charm to do this, but I do *not* mean in a sexual or sensual way.

In all dealings with people — face to face, telephone, or written — you are communicating, and so the *way* you communicate is the key to dealing with people.

Good communication

There are two parts to communication, verbal and non-verbal.

Verbal communication

The *content* of verbal communication is very important. Although it is only a part of what you communicate to somebody it is important that you do say exactly what you mean. You must make clear what you mean to say and then check that the listener has heard what you really mean to say by asking for feedback. For example if you ask somebody for a report 'as soon as possible' and then shout at them if it is not ready by the following morning, are you really being fair? As soon as possible may mean tomorrow to you but to somebody else it may mean next week.

As you must be aware, our minds often jump from one thing to another and what you actually say could be two or three stages on from the original meaning of your thoughts. It is important that what you say is your real intent. For example, the thought process may go 'I think I need a break — I think we need a way to get out of this room — we could go to the cafeteria — yes we could have a cup of coffee'. So you say to your colleague, 'let's have a cup of coffee' and he or she replies 'no thanks'. That only means that he does not want a cup of coffee, but that was not the original intention of your question. If you had said, 'I think we need a break, let's have a coffee or go for a walk or something' you may have got a very different answer.

Look at this problem: an employee is extremely meticulous with her work, to the extent where she is spending too much time on fine details which are irrelevant to the overall success of the project. What you want to do is to continue to get a good standard of work out of the employee but speed things up a little by cutting out these irrelevant details. That is your intent. If you go to that employee and you say, 'you are wasting too much time on detail. I want you to speed up and get down to the real job' do you think that will encourage her to work quicker? No, it is most unlikely to do so because she feels alienated and believes that you do not appreciate her care and attention to detail.

To get that employee on your side and then work together towards a solution you should first understand why she takes so much care and trouble over her work, she is probably trying to be the best at what she does, to be very efficient and to please you. To get that employee to understand what you really want you need to persuade her that she is really appreciated; for example a conversation that begins with a remark such as 'you know I really appreciate all the effort and attention to detail which you put into your projects and I know that you're trying to produce good results and be very efficient. But, we have some time constraints on this and there may be ways that we could speed up the work a little bit without detracting from your usual high standards. Perhaps we could try for a while leaving out refining the fine details and you could put your projects in to me at an earlier stage?' In this example, you have found out why the employee does what she does, you have empathized with her by congratulating her on a good job and then you have shown that you too care about what she produces by showing your interest in her intent before going on to make suggestions as how you can 'improve' what she does and therefore achieve your intent.

Non-verbal communication

Non-verbal skills include body language. Remember that I said in Chapter 3 that only 7 per cent of somebody's first impression is on what we say and 38 per cent on how we say it, but the other 55 per cent is based on how we look. How we look is not just the way we dress but the way we walk and carry ourselves and the mannerisms we have. Body language is a wide subject and there are a number of good books available on it — it is also fascinating and worth spending the time to read about it in more detail. However, there are a few key points you should take note of here:

- **Don't** use a 'little girl voice': it won't gain you sympathy, only ridicule and de-value what you are saying
- **Don't** smile too much: it is a sign of nervousness
- **Don't** tilt your head — stand or sit straight and look directly at the person you are dealing with
- **Don't** use nervous body movements such as crossing your legs while standing, nodding your head too often and fidgeting with jewellery, hair or clothes.

Remember, you can lose a lot of credibility by presenting yourself badly.

Establishing rapport

Establishing rapport with a colleague can be easier if you learn not only to listen to what they say but how they say it. People can be roughly grouped into those with three main preferences: visual, auditory, and kinesthetic (feelings). To establish rapport you need to understand which of these groups your colleague belongs to. There are two main methods of doing this, by looking at the words, especially verbs, that they choose, and the way their eyes move.

Listen for verbs which are predominantly in one of the three main groupings:

Visual	Auditory	Kinesthetic/Feelings
See	Listen	Feel
Look	Tell	Grasp
View	Discuss	Excite
Clear	Rings	That fits
Notice	Explain	Pick up on
Focus	Tune in	Strikes me as
Watch	Sounds	Seems
Show	Say	Handle
Observe	Hear	Smooth over
Appear		Touch

All these relate to their perception of things as do the way their eyes move when they are talking about something. The visual person looks up when they are talking, the auditory person tends to look towards the left or right, almost as if they were looking at their ears, and the person who works with feelings tends to look down — usually towards their right but this may vary, particularly if they are left handed.

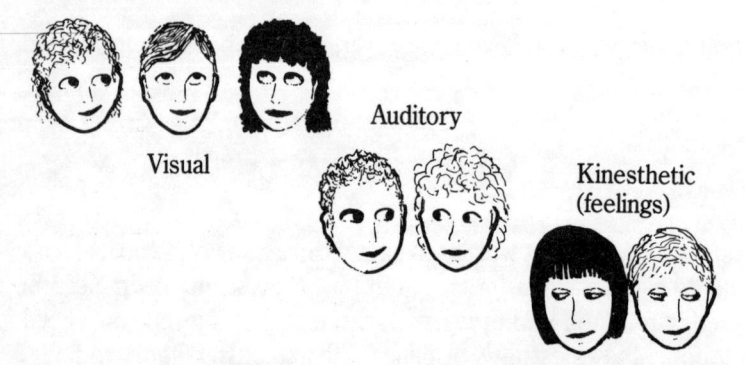

Visual   Auditory   Kinesthetic (feelings)

When you have worked out what type of person you are working with then you can use their preferred style in describing things and discussing points with them. If you are a person who usually deals with feelings but you are talking to a visual person, instead of saying, 'Yes, I feel that too' you may say, 'Yes, I see it that way too'. It takes a little practice not to make this seem stilted and unnatural, but it is surprising how much it can help somebody else to relate to you and is worth trying.

Giving information and being heard

As well as listening it is important that you are able to give information, and there may be occasions when the person you are giving it to appears to be listening but is not really hearing you. This may be a power play on their behalf, and done intentionally to make you feel unimportant or insecure. There are ways that you can tell that this is happening. For example, one way you can tell this is that their timing is out — they do not respond at the right time or in the right way to what you are saying. Another way is that they are apparently distracted easily by other things: they look around them, they look past you or at their watch or a clock; they make comments or gestures to other people walking by or in the room, or call their secretary in; they look at or read something which is on their desk, even signing a letter or a note while you are still talking; they take phone calls, either answering the phone as it rings on their desk immediately as if that is much more important than you, whoever is at the other end of the line, or accepting calls which the secretary puts through when they could be put off easily for a short time. These are all ways of saying to you that they consider themselves to be more powerful than you and what they have to do is more important than what you are trying to tell them. If you continue to sit there or stand there and talk while all these distractions are taking priority you are as good as agreeing that what they have to do or say is more important than you and therefore you are in a weak position. There are a number of ways in which you could deal with a situation like this:

Firstly, if what they are doing is very overt — for example taking several phone calls while you are talking, accepting interruptions from other people and so on — one thing you can do is to make a statement such as, 'this seems like a very busy time, I will come back later' and deliver to them a piece of paper with the information on and leave. This shows that you have realized what is going on and that you do not intend to be intimidated and ignored.

Secondly, if you want to continue the conversation/meeting, another ploy you can use is to use non-verbal communication skills to this individual. First and most powerful of these is silence — if you suddenly stop talking because they are not paying attention it will immediately grab their attention. Once they have looked up and you have their attention you could continue talking again at that point, but in fact that is not the most effective thing to do. Once you have got their attention you should sit and look directly at them but in silence, for as much as 3 to 5 seconds, and then finally when you do begin speaking again do not speak quickly or rush through it but speak slowly and deliberately in a powerful manner, thus emphasizing the importance of what you have to say.

However, there are those with whom this non-verbal technique does not work. You may have to try it once and discover that it is not working before you decide on a second ploy. In this situation you will have to use verbal skills as well. This technique again starts with silence when you have obviously lost their attention, then when you have gained their attention you make a statement such as, 'this seems to be a very busy time for you', or something similar: this is not threatening, you are merely stating what is, or appears to be, a fact. You should then state the importance of what you have to say, a phrase such as, 'I believe that this project is very important and we need to discuss it carefully', and finally you should suggest an alternative time, and length of time for another meeting, 'perhaps we can talk about it tomorrow morning, it will only take about half an hour of your time'. Having done this it is most unlikely that you won't get a commitment from that individual to give you the time you need, and because they know it will only take 30 minutes of their time they are likely actually to give you their attention. But it is very important that you stick to your 30 minutes, once you have used this ploy and failed by over-running the time you will not be able to use it again.

Make sure your communication skills are good. One skill used by good communicators is repetition. Frequent repetition of each point as it has been made or summarizing of points is a skill often used by powerful people. Another important tool for good communication is solicitation of feedback. Feedback is a key to good communication: in the end it is not what you said or the message you thought you put across which is important but what the recipient actually heard. You cannot automatically assume that once you say it, it has been heard and it will be done, the key to ensuring the correct action is to get feedback straight away, right there on the spot. Sometimes as women, we are too innocent in assuming that what we tell somebody has actually been heard, understood, and will be acted upon — make no assumptions that this is so. Even asking for feedback does not ensure that the correct action will be taken, and the way you ask for feedback is another important factor. If at the end of a statement or series of statements you say, 'Has everyone understood?' or 'Is that okay?' the likely reaction from people, especially those subordinate to you, is to say 'yes' even if that is not true. Asking if everyone, 'understands, okay?' is not good solicitation of feedback. You need to ask specific questions which will ensure that you know the recipient really understands what you have said and what you meant by it.

If you have a boss who does not solicit feedback or only gives a question which demands the answer 'yes' or 'no' then you will need to take the initiative. To do this you need to paraphrase what he or she has said and feed it back to them. For example, when the boss asks, 'Do you understand?' you should reply with a comment like, 'It seems to me that you require me to complete this report by such and such a date. Is that correct?' Obviously you will devise your own way of doing this, but it is important that it is made clear that you are clarifying for your own information, not in a manner threatening to your boss. By doing it this way, you are not putting your boss in a threatening situation and you are not being over-powering, but you are giving him or her the opportunity to clarify any points which were not clear. This may happen in more than one way or require more than one attempt before you are both sure that the other fully understands the situation and you have agreed what is to be done and when.

Dealing with difficult people

When we see people as being 'difficult' it is because there is a conflict between what they are doing and what you want. They are indulging in behaviour which we do not find acceptable. This means that we are part of the equation ourselves, and so have some ability to affect the way other people behave. Therefore when you are learning to deal with difficult people the first thing you are able to and need to change is your own behaviour. You may find this difficult because you may feel 'why should I change, they are the one who is wrong'. If they are wrong and a truly difficult person it is very unlikely that they will change unless something triggers it and that trigger can be a change in your own behaviour. So, no matter if it is distasteful to you, you must accept that your behaviour must change in order to change theirs. You need to be confident, calm and positive if you are to be effective in changing other people's behaviour. You must decide what you want and be specific about it and then work towards that goal. If you are in a situation that is not being productive then you must learn to be flexible to change that situation.

Pacing

The essence of pacing is to reduce the differences between you and another person and work towards the common ground. Pacing puts you both on the same side, and lays the foundation for working together towards a solution.

The first step is to get your body posture in rapport with the person you are dealing with, then you find the same rhythm as them (for example in their breathing or in the speed of which they are speaking), and finally you use similar gestures to theirs.

The next stage in pacing is the use of the voice, both in tone and speed. It is not essential that you exactly match your colleague's tone and speed, especially if your colleague is shouting rapidly in a high pitched tone! Use your tone in a calming manner and slow your pace a little behind theirs but not too much. The speed is even more important if you are speaking to a very slow speaker, because if you speak too quickly it is likely that not only will they lose rapport with you but they will miss what you say.

The last part of pacing is the verbal part, what you actually say.

One way of showing the listener that you are actually listening to what they say is by 'replaying' what they have just said back to them, not just paraphrasing as in feedback, but using the actual words that they have used to repeat what they have just said. This shows your listener that you have actually listened to and taken notice of what they were saying. In a normal situation you would confirm what somebody said by paraphrasing but in a conflict situation it is more likely to put you on common ground if you repeat back what they actually say, and then if you want to confirm what that meant to you, you can also paraphrase it in your own words. Remember that the important thing in a conflict situation is to meet on common ground.

Remember that in pacing what you are trying to do is build a rapport with the other individual, you are not trying to become them, so therefore be careful of 'over-doing' the pacing and possibly even appearing to mock them by exactly copying their gestures.

You have a right to be assertive

We will look at assertiveness in more detail in Chapter 7, but it is relevant here that you understand what it is, and more especially the two extremes of non-assertive behaviour, because these are often the causes of conflict between people of different personalities.

You are entitled to your opinion and in most circumstances there is no good reason why you should not express that opinion, (although sometimes for political reasons you may *choose* not to). If someone is preventing you from expressing an opinion then they are being difficult and making life difficult for you, so you should know how to find a way around that. You also have as much right to choose *not* to say what you think, or to say 'no' at any time, and again if someone else has prevented you from doing that they are being difficult and you should learn how to deal with it. In fact you have a responsibility to your organization to express your opinion and contribute your ideas. Your opinion is valuable and therefore you should be able to feel comfortable giving it.

Passive behaviour is either when you do not stand up for your rights at all, or when you do it in such a way that you are easily overcome and your rights are violated. This behaviour implies to someone else that you think, '**you're** okay and **you** have the right to do as you want but **I'm** not that important'. Aggressive behaviour is where you stand up for your rights in such a way that it is to the detriment of others. You are saying to them by this behaviour, '**I'm** okay, **I'm** important but what **you** think/say/do does not matter'. In the middle is an assertive person whose behaviour is signalling to others, '**I** may not be right, **you** may not be right, but let's work it out between us'.

The behaviour of a passive person is that his body language invites others to put him down and he will use a quiet hesitant voice which easily allows others to interrupt or argue with him. The behaviour of an aggressive person has over-exaggerated gestures, a defiant overpowering body posture and loud language which shouts other people down and doesn't listen to their comments. But there are degrees of this behaviour and the way in which you see another person's behaviour will depend upon the viewpoint from which you are looking. If you are a very passive, timid person, the behaviour of somebody who is no more than just assertive, may appear aggressive to you, if you are an over-aggressive person, the behaviour of anybody whom you can overpower may seem passive.

So, the basic premise of assertiveness is that you do have rights and you should be able to offer your opinion and have your say and to some extent do what you want, but not at the expense of others. You are looking to deal with other people on equal terms, with neither side dominating or defeating the other.

Identifying types of 'difficult' people

There are a number of reasons why people can be difficult, and a variety of ways in which they can be difficult to deal with, for example not only be being obstructive or refusing to carry out tasks but by also always agreeing with you and then never actually doing anything. If you can identify how and why these people are difficult to deal with then you can begin to overcome the problems.

It is possible to identify four main types of character: the directive, the analyst, the relator, and the expressive type.

The difficult people grid

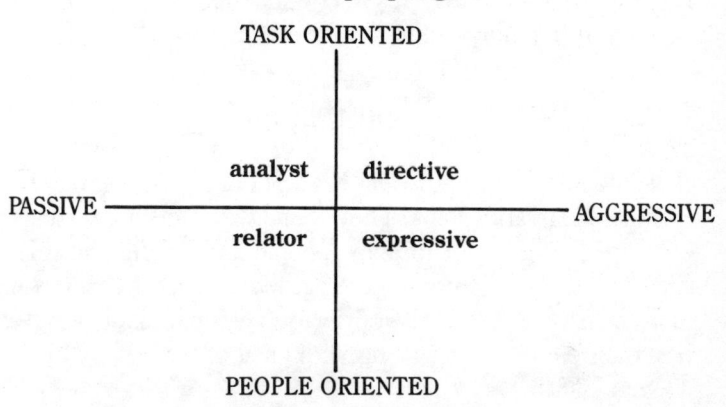

```
                TASK ORIENTED
                      |
            analyst   |  directive
PASSIVE ──────────────┼────────────── AGGRESSIVE
            relator   |  expressive
                      |
               PEOPLE ORIENTED
```

The archetypical examples of difficult people fit into the four quadrants of this grid, although few people will fit exactly into any one category. But first of all you should identify where *you* fit on this grid. When you understand where you are, it will help you to see how you relate to others.

The directive style

The directive person (North East quadrant) only wants to know the salient points, cuts out all the anecdotes and interesting asides, and wants to get straight to the point. He or she is very concerned about the task at hand, and about getting things done. These people are very efficient, very organized and excellent time managers. They always want you to get to the point, and get things done.

The analyst thinker

These people (the North West quadrant of the diagram) spend their time gathering information. They also have a task priority but they are more interested in the process involved in accomplishing the task than in actually achieving it. They usually organize their time well, but their pace is slow and they want the time to process the information and examine every detail. They make decisions and take actions slowly. This person needs you to be precise and accurate in the information you give him.

The relator

These people (the South West quadrant of the diagram) are most interested in relationships. They spend their time at meetings and seminars trying to get to know people and building up relationships with them. They are at the passive end of the assertiveness scale and have people as their priority. Their pace is slow and easy, they want people to get along with each other.

The expressive type

The expressive type (the South East quadrant of the diagram) are people-oriented. They like to be the centre of attention: they prefer to receive attention than to give it. They are at the more aggressive end of the assertiveness scale and are also people-oriented. Their real priority is with people at this moment, they pay attention to their immediate relationships at any time. They make decisions quickly, and they want what they contribute to any group or meeting to be appreciated.

If you can identify where you fit into these groups yourself it will help you to understand how you see others and how they see you. For example a directive type talking to another directive type will find agreement on getting things done quickly and decisively, but an analytical type will see a directive as too hasty.

What these people do and do not like

The **directive** type hates inefficiency and worries most about losing control. The **analytical** type gets most irritated by inaccurate information and is most worried about being caught being inaccurate. They do not like being wrong, and therefore do not like being rushed into decisions, or doing things without *all* the possible relevant information. In fact they do not really like making decisions at all, in case they may have missed out some vital piece of information. Because people are so important to the **relators** the greatest way to irritate them is by being insensitive or involving them in a conflict or confrontation situation. The **expressive** type does not like losing prestige or failing to get recognition for something he has done. They will go to great lengths to ensure they get recognition for the things they do. Another source of irritation to these people is boredom, they do not like things that are dull and uninteresting.

But as well as their dislikes, for each type of personality you can find things which they do like and which they will relate to, so you can 'pace' them, as well as deciding which things to avoid so you do not irritate them. With the **directive** put him in control; with the **analyst** be precise and accurate; the **relator** is seeking your approval and needs to know if he is on common ground with you, and the **expressive** needs to be recognized in front of others for what he is doing right.

None of these personalities is any better or any worse than any other. As an individual, each one may lack certain attributes, but very rarely do people work in isolation and therefore in any team or group you would want each of these people for the different attributes which they bring. However, putting these people together in a group could cause conflict — for example, a directive having to work with a relator could become irritated by the relator's lack of incentive to get things done, whereas the relator will become irritated with the directive who seems to care little about people's feelings. A really effective manager should be flexible enough to handle the needs of these individuals and make the best use of them.

If you can meet people where they are that is the key to reducing conflict in situations where the people appear to be difficult. When they are under stress or in what appears to be a conflict situation these people may become more difficult to handle because their characteristics become more exaggerated. It is then that your skills as a flexible manager are most needed.

Under stress — the directive

Under stress, the directive may appear blunt and pushy, critical and even overbearing. What they need is for you to move at their fast pace with them. You need to let them know that your intention is the same as theirs, i.e. to achieve their goals quickly and efficiently. When the directive sees things getting in the way of achieving his goals he can become irritated, frustrated and often rude. If you have to deal with a person in this situation you need to stand your ground, physically as well as mentally. You may need to give them time to run down, but if they carry on too long or have too much ammunition you may need to interrupt them. If you do this be firm but not aggressive about.

You need to pace them and work alongside them, not start an argument which you are quite likely to lose. What may appear to you to be their 'aggressive' behaviour is to them just their means of pushing forward and getting things done. Therefore you need to pace them and show them that you are interested in getting things done as well, but also to show them that there may be other considerations and ways of doing it. Your aim is also to get something done, but you need to put your point of view and perhaps alter the approach. To do this you need to be firm and assertive, but not aggressive.

It may not be your natural approach to stand up and discuss things with somebody who is attacking you verbally, but only by doing that will you overcome their perception of you as being weak and inadequate. By standing up and demonstrating your strength and your commitment to a result you are showing them that you have something to contribute which is worth listening to. You must be brief, to the point, and well prepared. In this way you are pacing them by showing them that you too want a result which achieves something positive.

Dealing with interruptions

A tactic of the directive type is using interruptions, they will keep interjecting remarks which throw doubt on what you were saying or cause a cheap laugh at your expense. They do this because they wish they were in control but because they are not their tactics are to knock your feet from under you. They surround themselves with the protection of the group and their social norms, at your expense. People who do this either wish to call attention to themselves, genuinely do not agree with what you have to say, or want to gain their advantage at your expense.

To overcome this problem you need to bring the grievance to the surface and deal with it. You can do this by calling attention to the sarcasm, and then provide a peaceful alternative to the conflict. Ask the interrupter questions, rather than making assumptions or assertions. If there are others present you can also involve the group, thus helping you to broaden the issue and get useful feedback. Do this by finding out whether or not they agree or disagree with the criticism: if they disagree that will usually put an end to the interrupter's accusations. It may also be necessary for you to define the problem, and find out what the root cause of the interruptions is. The interrupter will be offering you solutions or alternatives but not actually telling you what his or her problem is. To do this you need to find out all the information about their problem by asking them questions and then problem-solve with the individual or the group to sort out the difficulty. Sometimes the interrupter will try to align with the group against you — your best course of action in this situation is to reaffirm the purpose of the meeting or your contribution and ask the interrupter how their contribution is going to help with this.

Dealing with 'steamrollering' directives

These are people who think they know all the answers. This person will frequently stand over you and constantly give you a negative feedback on what you are doing. You need to get this individual to consider your alternatives.

Although they may have a lot of the right answers they probably don't have all the information, and what you have to contribute may be critical to the success of the project or the job. You need to persuade them to listen to your part. In order to do this, first of all you must be sure you are knowledgeable; do your homework properly and then when you are sure you have all the information listen to their contributions and opinions first. Then when you have paced them and they believe you are listening to them offer your ideas and approaches, but presenting these as possible theories of optional approach, for example 'What about if we did xyz?' , or 'If we try so and so now, what will happen in the future?'

It is not worth arguing head-to-head with this person but better to listen to them and offer your opinion. As a last resort you may have to accept their point of view and the fact that they will not listen to yours, but hope that they will take on board some of what you have said.

Under stress — the analytical type

Under stress, the analyst may become withdrawn and resentful, resistant to change and unable to meet deadlines. This is because he is after total accuracy, but the world is not that simple and is under constant change. Because he is a slow decision maker, feeling under stress when he does not have all the information he believes he needs, he may become unable to make decisions at all.

People like this will have a great deal of information to offer and need to be listened to, and to help them you must support their process of information gathering and giving by listening to them. If you give them responsibility for accuracy and information you will please them and reduce their stress levels.

Dealing with complaints

Your aim in dealing with someone who is complaining is to get them to switch from *complaining* about their problems to *solving* their problems. They are obviously aware of problems, that is the source of their complaint, but they seem to be totally unable to do anything about them. Their tactic is to try to throw their problem at you and expect you to do something about it. Complaining is a defence mechanism against blaming themselves for something that has not worked out right. By telling you their problem, i.e. complaining, they are trying to put the onus on you to solve it.

To get them to switch to problem solving themselves the first thing you have to do is listen attentively to their problem. When you think you have understood the main points, you will need to interrupt them and backtrack by using feedback to make sure that you have got the main points. Then you will need to ask questions, but limiting questions that will avoid the sweeping generalizations this type of person usually uses.

Questions such as, 'Exactly *who* in this case?' or 'Can you give me an example of that?' are useful. Avoid asking 'Why?' as this will give them an excuse to start again — your questions should be simple and closed. Do not agree with the complainer, but state facts without comment: this can lead into problem solving, where you ask questions about specific points. Assign tasks to the complainer, for example gathering further information on a specific topic. Finally if nothing else works you must ask them how they would like the discussion to end and set a time limit on the discussion.

Sometimes a complainer will complain about a third party — the best way to deal with this is to ask them if they have told that person what their problem is. If they agree to do this you can suggest that they get together and solve the problem jointly, but it is most likely that they will be unwilling to confront the third party. In that instance, you could suggest that you may tell that person what the complaint is. If the complainer is willing for you to pass on the information make sure you do have the specific facts by asking questions as before. Vague generalizations are likely to lead to bad feelings and misunderstandings. If the complainer is not willing for you to talk to the third party on their behalf then you should throw the ball back into their court with a remark such as, 'Well, let me know when you change your mind'. You do not want to be left as the one holding the problem.

Dealing with the negative thinker

The problem with someone who is always negative about everything is that they probably actually believe that the situation is hopeless. They may even subconsciously be trying to protect you from disappointment by holding you back from making mistakes. Use their negative comments as useful warning signs, and pay attention to them, but do not get dragged down into their negative way of thinking. It is useful to obtain all the information and facts but you do not need to argue with these people, this is only likely to distract you from your cause or intent. You may find others who are swayed by their arguments, but if you genuinely believe in what you are doing you may have to go it alone and assert your right to your own opinions and decisions.

Under stress — the relator

When these people get stressed they appear passive, indecisive and defensive. The most upsetting thing for these people is insensitivity and confrontation. They need you to slow down the pace when they are under stress, and give them comfort and reassurance that the relationship is good and they are liked.

Dealing with stalling tactics

Someone who stalls will constantly put off decisions, usually because these may have negative effects and they do not want to hurt anybody or they cannot face up to the consequences of their decisions. To overcome this problem you need to 'make it safe' for them to be honest and help them move forward by reassuring them that your relationship is good and will be improved by honesty. By asking for their consideration but continuing to reassure them you can have an honest dialogue with them. Then you can move on to help them examine the facts and problem-solve the issues. You can do this through giving them support while they air the possible alternatives, but you may in the end need to take the action steps yourself.

If the problem that this person has is related to you, and they do not want to do or say something because of its affect on you, you need to work hard at reassuring them and to try to get them to tell you why they are uneasy about the decision or the action. You need to get them to commit themselves to an action, and make sure that you reaffirm this by reinforcing the statement — for example, 'Now you will do xyz in future won't you?' If they avoid confirming what you have said you may need to explore the issue further.

Dealing with the 'agreeable' person

Some people can cause problems because they will agree to anything, and you never find out what their real concerns are. You have probably come across a person who when you ask them something answers with, 'I don't mind, do what you want to'. The end result of this can be that you both end up doing something you don't want to do or that nothing actually gets done at all. This person may not want to risk the chance of you getting upset if they say 'no', so they will *agree* to do something but because they don't really want to they never actually carry it out. They say 'yes' at that moment because they want to avoid a potential confrontation, but they don't think about what will happen later and how they may have to explain a job not done.

What you need to do is understand this problem and get them to realize that it is best if they are honest now rather than waiting for the repercussions later. You need to reassure them, and have an honest dialogue by asking questions which lead them to think about a future, but at the same time reassuring them about the relationship now. Next you need to air the issue involved and get them to realize the positive consequences of making a decision or carrying out an action. Finally make sure that you reinforce their commitment actually to doing something before you leave the topic.

There are a lot of similarities between the agreeable person and the staller, and the common way of dealing with them is to reassure them and put them in a situation where they feel safe, have an honest dialogue, and then bring the problems to the surface and work together to solve the issues. This will help you to understand what stops people achieving things so you can work together to overcome this problem; it is much better than having projects completed late or reports not delivered when you need them without understanding why.

Under stress — the expressive

Under stress these people will appear to be superficial, over-eager and manipulative. Their greatest worry is losing prestige or self-esteem, and you are most likely to antagonize them by making fun of them in front of people they wish to impress. They need someone to give them some recognition and credit when they are under stress, which means that you must look for the positive intent in what they are doing.

Dealing with the person who loses control

When someone gets upset or loses control then your approach must be to help them gain their self control. To do this first of all you need to gain their attention but at the same time show that you are concerned about them by using a statement such as 'I like your idea but . . .'. And you may need to suggest that you have a short break while things calm down.

Dealing with a know-it-all

This person may not actually 'know-it-all', but they do believe that they do. One type of know-it-all is one that comes out with all sorts of crazy ideas but because they present them so well they appear to be workable. Your aim must be to show that these ideas are unworkable but not at the expense of the prestige of that individual. You could do this by suggesting that you have some information which they may not have seen yet, but not in a challenging or aggressive way.

You need to give them a way out so that they can go along with your ideas but still save face. You can do this by stating facts and giving them a chance to escape, because as soon as they realize that you do know what you are talking about they are likely to be looking for a way out. If you do not give them a way out they may have to defend themselves by becoming firmer on their position and making it more difficult for you.

Being flexible

Generally, dealing with difficult people involves altering your behaviour which will enable them to alter theirs. You may have to do what you would least like to do in any situation in order to move towards the middle ground where you can meet them and solve your conflict. This is not a sign of weakness but a sign of a good flexible manager who can see the problems and is prepared to work towards solving them.

Flexibility means adapting to change and being able to cope with new situations. Women are frequently accused of not being flexible, and particularly of not being able to cope with a crisis. In fact this is usually untrue — frequently in our day-to-day domestic lives and throughout our upbringing we have had to cope with crises in a wide variety of situations and have coped well with them. Perhaps our reputation of not being able to deal with a crisis stems from our natural expressiveness where we will show the emotion of distress or concern when things do not go as we please. That does not mean we are not coping, it just means we are showing our concern, but to male colleagues it is not seen like this. Thus we are frequently damned as being inflexible when the real problem is that we are not showing control. Not only must we learn control but we must learn to have contingency plans for situations which will change. People who make it to the top will have lots of choices available to them through making all kinds of strategy and plans.

Fighting battles

Women still find it difficult to compete and even harder to fight. Our upbringing teaches us that we should be pleasant, soft, quiet, and approved of and so we are uncomfortable when challenging others. Being too accommodating undermines the image of strength which is needed for success at work.

Organizations do not exist for the benefit of their employees, organizations exist to produce profit or return on investment. You are being paid to do a job. Women managers often feel that their prime purpose is to look after the interests of their people. While this is laudable, this is not what they exist for. If you must fight a battle pick a battle you can win. Don't alienate your boss by suddenly trying to change things that have been done the same way for years just because you believe it is morally wrong. The track record of executives in winning battles is probably only 51 per cent; you will have to accept that you will lose some battles, but maximize the probability of winning by choosing the right battles to fight. You cannot fight every battle as it comes indiscriminately. This is another example of focusing your energy on the right goals.

It is sometimes worthwhile, when you feel like rushing out and fighting a battle, to go away to sleep on it then decide: firstly, do you really want to fight this battle? and then, if you are going to take it up, what is the most rational way to do so?

Do not fight your battle emotionally, plan your strategy and make sure you are on firm ground. Do not fight battles on feelings, make sure you gather the facts, the figures and the information you need to put your case rationally and sensibly.

Have a sense of humour

Having a sense of humour is a weapon of self-defence. If you can make your opponent laugh you can win every time.

Women have a tendency to take themselves too seriously, they also take all that is happening around them too seriously. The ability to see the funny side of something or to make a humorous comment at a meeting can be a powerful ploy. It should be used with care — do not make jokes at someone else's expense, and do not try to tell set-piece jokes. A spontaneous humorous comment can be very welcome and sometimes can even defuse a potential conflict situation.

Speaking up and being heard

Having good communication skills and understanding how to handle individuals is only part of the battle. You must also learn how to speak up and be heard and learn what you need to say to impress.

You must learn how to participate in meetings and how to organize and run meetings. You must also learn how to speak with authority by using the right jargon associated with your business.

We will look at this again in Chapter 6.

Handling pressure

Being a manager in any organization is hard: being a woman manager is even harder. Therefore in addition to your business skills you must also learn how to cope with the stresses and how to switch off and recharge your batteries.

Before you can learn to control your stress you need to know what causes it. As a quick 'consciousness raiser' look at the list below. It is intended to help you recognize some of the conditions that determine your level of stress. Next to each statement give a number from 0 to 5 as follows: 0 = never; 3 = sometimes; 5 = habitually.

- I have a lot on my mind that worries me — at work, at home or both. ☐
- My family makes too many demands on me. ☐
- I don't have enough time for leisure and to take care of personal needs. ☐
- I handle most things alone with little support from my family or colleagues. ☐
- I have too much responsibility. ☐
- I have trouble focusing on a task. ☐
- I have difficulty communicating with my children, family, boss or colleagues. ☐
- I do not have enough say in decisions that affect me. ☐
- There is a great deal of time pressure at work. ☐
- I am often tired. ☐
- People or things often irritate me. ☐
- I regularly have headaches (score 5 for twice a week or more often). ☐
- I have muscle tension in my shoulders, neck or back. ☐

- There is considerable illness in my life, either myself or my family. ☐
- I regularly have a drink to wind down. ☐
- I drink a great deal of coffee or other caffeine drinks. ☐
- My family or friends or people at work tell me that I drink too much. ☐
- I smoke. ☐
- Most of my time is spent sitting, I get little exercise. ☐
- My life is one crisis after another. ☐
- I would like to make changes in my life but don't know how. ☐
- I have very high standards for myself. ☐

TOTAL: ___

What is your total score? Read the explanations below:

Under 25: You seem to be coping well and don't have any major stresses.

25 - 45: This is average but you could lower your stress levels.

46 - 65: You should be thinking seriously about making changes in your life.

Over 65: You must act now to reduce your stress levels.

This is neither scientific nor conclusive but it will have raised your awareness of your situation, helping you to consider whether you do need to make changes and make life less stressful for yourself. Research has shown that work overload is the leading stressor for women in most western countries, although many acknowledge that this is self-imposed because they work harder than men in order to prove themselves. Other high stresses are deadlines and time pressures, situations over which individuals do not have any control, conflict between work, home and social life, and poor interpersonal relationships.

Many of the problem areas for women managers (especially feelings of lack of confidence, difficulties in being assertive or delegating, and the need to be liked and respected at work) are found primarily at the junior and supervisory to middle management levels. Presumably the higher up the managerial hierarchy you go the better you have mastered these problems.

You should regard symptoms of stress positively as early warning signals, and do something about them. It is also important that you count your blessings and look on the bright side. Start by reviewing your values, make sure that you are not putting yourself under unnecessary pressure by confusing your priorities. Accept what cannot be changed, have the courage to change what can be changed, and the wisdom to know the difference. Before you decide that something cannot be changed look at it carefully and decide if it really cannot be changed or if it is just that you lack the courage to do it. Don't be afraid to discuss things with others, particularly in areas of conflict. Discussing something at an early stage can help to relieve it before it becomes acute.

Make the best use of your energy and pay proper attention to your health. Balance work with recreation and set aside time each day to relax and reflect. Diet and relaxation are two important keys to good health, the other is exercise. If you are worried about your health get a health check-up and discuss your diet and exercise with your doctor. A fitter person is not only more energetic and capable but if you are fit you will find it much easier to cope with minor irritations. Taking time out to get fit is time well spent and will pay you dividends in the long run. You have probably been through the situation where you struggle to work with a streaming cold, feeling awful, and wished you had not gone. If you take a day off to make yourself better and then go back feeling fit you are capable of getting through much more work and you know that it will be more efficiently and effectively handled.

Read a good book on nutrition and improve your diet, taking less fats, sugars, salt, alcohol, and caffeine. Eat more fresh vegetables, fibre and low-fat products. It may be difficult with business lunches and grabbing meals at odd times but when eating out most menus now will provide a salad and you don't *have* to eat the gateau for sweet! If it is difficult to get away for lunch take a small lunch box with you containing some fresh fruit or a salad and make yourself go away from your desk for at least fifteen minutes — the break will leave you feeling refreshed and much more willing to work.

Remember making yourself ill is not going to do you, your company, or your career prospects any good: a lot of thought and a small amount of time and effort making yourself fit are really worth while.

If, like me, you spend most of your working day sitting at your desk, in someone else's office, or in your car, then you have to make a positive effort to take some exercise. This is not always easy and is maybe something you have to *make* yourself do. One idea is to join a good leisure club — having paid the expensive fee you are not going to waste it by not using the facilities, are you? Also the relaxing atmosphere and pleasant surroundings to enjoy after you have exercised are likely to help to unwind you more. Joining a class or group is another way of making yourself take some regular exercise, but this may be more difficult if you travel a lot and are unable to meet at a regular time each week. Whenever possible when I am travelling I book into a hotel with a pool and get up early and have a swim before breakfast. It may seem like masochism at the time but it makes me feel really good afterwards.

Planning and control

At work you should face squarely anything that worries you and identify honestly the worst that could happen — this will help to release your anxieties. You *will* make mistakes, but use negative experiences as positive steps for learning, not episodes to look back on with regret. And finally, check your management skills. Don't set yourself unrealistic deadlines: order your priorities, delegate efficiently, and approach tasks methodically. Learn to plan and organize more effectively, include all the possible problems into your planning, and whenever possible do things in plenty of time as last minute rushes are not only stressful but also inefficient. Go on a time management course, even a one-day seminar can be a great benefit to helping you organize your time.

You will learn to do the important things first, to make lists of 'what to do' and prioritize your tasks. Working more effectively and efficiently is much more sensible than just working harder. As the Americans say 'Work smarter — not harder!'

If you are in charge of projects, learn project management techniques. You do not need a complex computer system for project management, at its simplest it is a series of common sense techniques which will help you to plan and control projects. Time spent planning at the outset will pay untold dividends during the project and enable you to set realistic deadlines which you can meet within your budget and resources.

If you are involved in events which have a high stress potential, then plan for them. Think of the problems and things that could go wrong and make contingency plans, for example take a spare machine, or bulb for the projector, take additional notes, take another key with you and so on.

If you are facing a problem, don't talk about the problem, focus on the end result. Ask yourself, 'What results do I want?' and then decide how you are going to get those results, by delegating, negotiating, or modifying your expectations. If none of these is possible then restate the problem and go back to the question, 'what results do I want?'

Emotions

Negative emotions are another stressor and learning to control these can help to reduce stress. If the emotion is anger (yours or other people's) first stop and breathe carefully, then ask yourself what results you want and create alternative solutions. If the negative emotion is a bad mood because a situation seems difficult, ask yourself the question, 'what's good about this situation?' and do not allow yourself the answer, 'nothing!' Look at the best thing that is available to you and what is good about it and build on that.

Keep yourself in check

A small amount of stress occasionally is a facet of most people's working lives, but constant or high stress is not desirable. If you are concerned, a talk with your doctor is needed. This book has only been able to touch on a complex and vital subject. Remember you are only part of the organization — your boss, colleagues, subordinates, and customers or clients are also part of the equation. Considering how you relate to and react with them could be an important first step in reducing your stress levels.

Chapter Six

Key Skills for Success in Business

Women's key skills

Women already possess a great many good management skills — the legacy of our upbringing and society's expectations of us is not all bad — but we do need to know how to use those skills, and then fill in the gaps with new skills when we need them. Ironically it is sometimes our own good work that gets in our way. We are conscientious but are often surprised and angry to discover that hard work and skill are not necessarily rewarded with pay rises and promotions. The higher you go in the work place the more your success depends on combining competence with political ability, a sense of strategy and human relationship skills. Going on a management course to gain skills not only gives you those management techniques but also often has the added bonus of giving you much more confidence in yourself.

Janet Rubin said, 'Many of the skills that women have are very unglamorous, things like working very hard and being very conscientious. But whatever skills you have these are greatly enhanced by anything which gives you credibility to overcome initial prejudice — for example good qualifications can get you in the door but once you are there you have to prove your worth.'

Geraldine Bown suggested, 'We have many skills which have been learned in the home as well as many natural abilities which can be used to great advantage in management.' Geraldine Bown believes that we should use and develop our strengths and not try to turn into male clones. 'Women who have had families and run homes have a number of home-based management skills which they can transfer to the work place. These include parallel processing (the ability to think about and carry out a number of different tasks at once); acting as a facilitator to encourage self-development; settling conflicts and problem solving with our families; we are also capable of crisis management, and time management, and are generally very flexible.' These are all skills which can be transferred to the work place to great advantage.

Clare Gallagher agrees, 'Women do have certain skills which they can bring to the management role, for example they are better at listening' but she also warns, 'Many of the home-based skills which women develop while they are home-makers or mothers are not valued by male managers if they are quoted in an interview situation. Men generally do not value the experience that home-making brings in management terms.'

Listening

Possessing active listening skills is an attribute towards surviving in business but is not one which we will address here in detail because women have traditionally been good listeners. It is interesting that men need more training in listening skills than women. Listening is a very powerful tool which women already have but do not make the best use of. They do not always make use of what they hear to their own benefit.

Geraldine Bown works as a training consultant and has found listening very important in her work, 'Women listen better and more effectively than men and in a consultancy role this is particularly helpful. It means that you are more likely to offer your clients a realistic, tailor-made result than an off-the-peg solution.' Also some women have found it easier to get people to talk to them because they are not as threatening or as competitive and hard-hitting as a man: a woman is more willing to relax and share in a discussion with other people.

Communicating

Women are very good communicators and generally have better vocabularies than men. Our background and upbringing leads us to express ourselves and speak about how we feel — not only in what we speak, but also in non-verbal communication. A word of caution, though — when you think about this in a business sense and the importance of control this can be a problem. In business a 'poker face' can be very useful. Sometimes women complain that they are not asked for their opinion in meetings. The automatic conclusion is that it is because you are a woman and therefore your colleagues think that your opinion is not important. While this may sometimes be the case, it could also be that with your non-verbal communication you are already giving them your opinion without speaking. As women we generally say and feel too much and those feelings and opinions are too readily expressed, frequently even without speaking. If you want to be consulted, and to give your considered opinion, then withhold this non-verbal information — use the 'poker face'.

Further female attributes

Women tend to have the ability to **read other people's body language.** This can be very useful, and powerful, but should be used carefully. For example, if in a meeting someone puts on a straight face and chooses not to comment on something, but their body language says they are anti, you do not let on that you have noticed that. If someone especially in a position of power, is trying to hide their feelings from the group, to realize that you can see through it can be very threatening for them. Store the information and use it in the future, but don't talk about it.

Anne Dixson feels that women are **good team builders,** perhaps rooted in the home-making role where the wife organizes games and activities for the family. This also develops the ability of a woman to motivate, give due recognition, reinforce and have good communication skills.

One of the things that we are good at is that we are **good at planning** and frequently have the foresight to realize all the different stages that need to go into achieving a particular goal. Sometimes when working towards a project we almost subconsciously know the sequence of events and do things in the right order to achieve our end result. Being used to somebody else picking up the pieces and carrying out some of the tasks for them, men do not always remember all the little things that need to go into completing a project successfully, and often end up at the last minute trying to get other people to help them sort things out.

Too much of a good thing?

However, because we do have certain skills as women we tend to take on too much work ourselves, and not leave it to others. Women are very efficient and very productive; research has shown that in general women work 50 per cent longer hours than their male counterparts. However, this does not necessarily mean that women are always effective workers. *Efficient* may be getting things done yourself, *effective* is getting them done by using other people to do them. We must be seen to be effective and good managers as opposed to efficient and well organized.

In an administrative and secretarial position the ability to cope with lots of different things at once is a great advantage, and this is a skill which many women have. But it can also be our downfall. Anne van der Salm says, 'Yes, I agree that I am good at coping with lots of different things at once, but sometimes we are not assertive enough to say "no"; we are always trying to help people and "be nice" but this can sometimes lead to us taking on more than we can realistically cope with'.

What managements skills do you need?

At the most senior levels it is not necessary to know every fine detail of how you put together the product that the company makes, but a senior manager should be in a position to have a broad over-view of the whole company and what every department is doing, to know how these fit together and plan strategies. At middle management levels and upwards, you are going to be evaluated on how you perform the management skills, not on the old technical skills which you started with. The following are some of the key management skills.

1. *Planning and organizing*: Traditionally as women we have been well organized, for years and throughout our upbringing we have organized other people. What we are less good at is planning.

2. *Delegation*: This is taking something which is your responsibility and giving or 'delegating' it to another party to carry out. As women we are frequently accused of not delegating well; while this is true, it is also true of many male managers.

3. *Problem solving and decision making*: This is the ability to work through problems systematically and come up with sensible and workable solutions. It also means that you must be able to make decisions about what to do. As women we are often quite good at problem solving, but frequently shy away from making decisions.

4. *Knowledge/Information*: About the product, the company and the politics. As women we tend to know about the product and the company well, we do our homework and we have that knowledge, but we do not know the political game well. The higher up you go the more your job is the politics.

Look at the skills you have — go back to the lists you made in Chapter Two and add to them any new ones which you had not thought of then and may have realized you have as you have read the earlier chapters of this book. Then think about where you need to fill the gaps. The following sections of this chapter will deal with some of these techniques which you will need to master.

Planning

There are four different levels of planning, the lowest level is short-term planning and scheduling other people or yourself in predetermined tasks: this is mainly *supervisory* level planning. If you are planning over a year ahead this is considered to be *tactical* planning and is the higher level in the hierarchy. If you are planning three to five years ahead, this is *strategic* planning: for most of us this will be the highest level of planning we will reach. But there is a higher level which is only used by a few and that is *systemic* planning, i.e. planning for a whole system. This means deciding what industries and whole areas of industry will be doing by sitting on major national bodies, etc.

Delegation

One of the skills we must use is delegation. Some women are good at it because it is the only way you can run a home and a career; working mothers have developed the art of delegation at home, but frequently forget how to do it when at work.

Women certainly have a tendency to take on too much and in the early stages of a career do not delegate willingly. This comes with experience and your willingness to delegate may depend on the team you have around you. It is good to assess their skills and use them where they have expertise but it is also important that you give them opportunities to develop and grow.

Anne Dixson feels that, unlike many women, she is able to delegate but finds it difficult to delegate to people who perform badly and would not persevere with them. However, when she does delegate a task to someone, she spends time explaining it and gives a lot of feedback to them about the task, a key to good delegation.

To delegate effectively you need to remember a few simple rules. Firstly you must ruthlessly analyse your abilities and the limits of your time, so that you can identify what can best be delegated. Re-examine the tasks you find particularly easy — it may be appropriate to delegate these as well as the tasks that you don't want to do. By delegating these tasks you can leave yourself free to do the work that only you can do.

Don't delegate the special tasks, such as vital tasks that only you can do in time to the required standard; those where confidentiality or a particular sensitivity is required; new or ill-defined tasks that a subordinate may not be able to organize easily.

Remember to delegate tasks in line with the skills of your subordinates and make sure that they receive the training necessary to do the job. You will need to keep a degree of control appropriate to the skills of the subordinate doing the task and check their progress to ensure that the tasks are being completed. Delegating does require courage, good judgement as to who is the best person for the job and how much help they need, and faith in others, but you must give the delegatee all the help you can. Clearly define the task you are delegating and make sure that the person who is carrying it out knows exactly what is expected of them. Ask them to give you feedback to be sure that they know what they should be doing, and make yourself available to help when and if necessary.

Delegating decision-making jobs also requires that you delegate the authority to get the job done. Make sure that your subordinate knows that you are backing him or her and give them the support they need. Use the delegation of important tasks to enrich your subordinate's job, improve his or her performance and therefore raise morale.

Productive thinking, problem solving and decision-making

Women need to develop more adult logical thinking. Liz Clarke said we should ask ourselves, 'What do I want in this situation?' and be honest about it. She suggests, 'Most women would rather take care than take charge, but it is acceptable to take charge at times and we should do it more often.' Many organizations are very autocratic and although some are moving towards a more participatory style there are occasions where you need to be decisive. In these situations it is always useful, as well, to have a fallback, i.e. a plan A and a plan B in case it doesn't work out. This contingency planning is something that women often do well.

It is possible to train yourself to think more productively and to structure your thinking to make the best use of it. We think both consciously and subconsciously; some of the best ideas come when we are not trying. Learn to recognize how your subconscious mind works so that you will be ready for ideas when they surface. Write down these ideas when they occur, even if it is in the middle of the night. Set aside a period each day for mental reflection, by dismissing the trivia of the day your mind is cleared and can be creative. At the end of the day make a list of priorities for the next day; don't wait until the morning, if you make these the night before your subconscious mind can be working on them overnight.

As well as making use of your subconscious, your conscious thinking can be more productive if you identify your most productive period of the day. Concentrate on managing well the hours when you are most productive and use this time for your most important work. Ensure that you have put enough time into analysing projects and gathering information so that your subconscious mind can work on these while you are doing other things. When you run into a dead end on a project, stop and check that you have got all the facts, that you have a starting point, that you have a perspective on the project, and that you are motivated. Analyse past successes and identify the reasons for failures so you can use these lessons productively. By using these techniques you will improve the way you think and make better use of your time.

When you have to solve a problem or make a decision it may seem so impossible or difficult that you put it off. There is a proverb which says: 'All problems are difficult before they are easy'.

Procrastination will never get anything done and the problem will remain with you and niggle at you for a long time. If you have a logical and structured approach then it is a way to get you started as well as the route to your solution.

As with your thinking time, use the part of the day when you are most productive and allocate some of this time to the problem. When you look at the problem start by defining the desired outcome, and write this down. Then state the problem clearly, half the solution of a problem is understanding what it is. Explaining the problem to someone else or writing it down will force you to clarify it and may be the beginning of solutions. Make sure at this stage that you have gathered all the information necessary, and if not, go away and collect what information you need before you continue. If the problem is complex or has a number of facets, start with the parts of the problem that seems easy or obvious, that way you will feel you are making progress and it will encourage you to continue. Think about, identify, and make a list of all the possible solutions then dismiss any that, for whatever reason, are not feasible. Finally, if you are sure that you have all the necessary input and can't see the solution, make a conscious decision to leave it for a while and your subconscious mind will work on it.

Sometimes problems will solve themselves or subsequent events will make it clear what course should be taken; it is quite legitimate to decide not to make a decision but you must *decide* not to decide, not just let it drag on.

If the problem or potential problem is one of conflict with a person then a different approach is needed. There are four steps which will be effective in confronting the conflict and dealing with it, the detail of how you use them is up to you to adapt to your own personal style.

To solve the problem you need to talk to the individual who is the cause of it and then take them through this process:

1. *What is happening?* — make a description of the other person's words and actions but do not include any judgments or conclusions.

2. *Results* — describe to them what the outcome or results of their behaviour will be; this may be in terms of time, money, energy, or resources.

3. *Feelings* — describe the negative emotions you have about the other person's behaviour.

4. *Request* — having explained the problem as you see it, make a specific request, for example 'Will you . . .' asking the other to change their behaviour.

During this process you must be prepared to listen actively. Depending on the problem and your position you may need to plan follow-up; if you do, be specific and definite about the follow-up and then make sure you do it. During the process you must be assertive but tactful and respectful, once the problem has been dealt with don't carry a grudge or continue to bring it up, let the individual learn that once a problem is aired it can be solved and then forgotten.

The right information/knowledge

Information is the key to powerful communication skills, not only giving information but also knowing when to withhold it. As women we are often, rightly, accused of giving away too much. We must learn when to give and when to withhold.

But we should also learn not to withhold information in an overpowering way. This means letting people know you have information but telling them you have chosen not to tell them what it is. That is overpowering. Sometimes you need to withhold information for good reasons, and people may know that you have that information, therefore you need to tell them that you cannot tell them, but the important difference is how you handle that. If you explain considerately to them the reasons why you cannot divulge the information, what you are doing about it and when they will know, this will enable them to accept more readily their own lack of knowledge and feel more understanding towards you and your position rather than feeling irritated or even aggressive.

Understanding and using jargon

Each particular field has its own language and jargon. If you are in a meeting with people who are constantly using terms you do not understand, you know how vulnerable this can make you feel. It is important that in your job you learn and use the terms appropriate to your field. Showing that you have a knowledge of and can use these terms establishes you as knowledgeable and therefore powerful in your field. Women frequently have not been good at learning about and using certain terms, particularly financial ones.

Financial jargon

The financial terms are keys to business and it is important that you learn them. The reason for the existence of any company is 'the bottom line', i.e. how much profit it makes at the end of the day. Showing that you understand and can use financial terms shows that not only are you interested in the people and the product, but also in the reason for that company's existence — the bottom line.

Many of the financial terms are given as initials or acronyms and may look daunting at first, but again most can be reduced to simple expressions or equations. Some of the main ones are given overleaf.

Understanding the jargon is one thing — using financial data is another. In fact company finance is much easier to understand than accountants would have us believe. The purpose of accounting is to provide records of all financial transactions, so that the financial position of a business can be determined. The accounts can then be used to produce reports showing the financial position for the owners or managers of the business and any other interested parties. The 'financial position' means: the surplus of profit generated; the cash position; a statement of wealth at a particular time including the assets of the business, any amount owed to others, and any amount owed to the business by others.

We are in business to create wealth, and 'wealth' is the possessions or assets of a company or individual. In order to create wealth the company or individual must own more assets at the end of a period of time than they did at the start. The amount of wealth created in a period is the retained profit.

Therefore profit represents both the sum remaining from trading and investment after all debts have been paid, and the difference between the wealth at the start of a period and the

ALOE	Assets = Liability + Owner's Equity.
AT	Asset Turnover = Total Sales Over Total Assets.
BUDGET	A budget is a plan expressed in financial terms. Where the key management tasks are: PLAN — IMPLEMENT — CONTROL, the matching financial roles are: BUDGET — RECORD — EVALUATE.
P/E	The price/earnings ratio = price per share over earnings per share. This ratio is widely quoted with the share listings in the papers and is probably the best representation of the feelings of the stock market about that company.
PGI	Profit growth index (%) = This year's profit over last year's profit.
ROCE	Return on capital employed (%) = Profit before interest and tax over total capital employed.
ROE	Return on equity or investors' ratio = Shareholders' earnings over shareholders' equity.
ROI	Return on investment.
ROS	Return on sales, or sales profitability (%) = Profit before interest and tax over total sales.
SGI	Sales growth index (%) = This year's sales over last year's sales.

wealth at the end (not including any capital which is injected by investors).

To create wealth we need to please our customers through good quality and delivery on time at the right price; we need to produce and sell efficiently; we need to keep those who have lent us money — e.g. banks or investors — happy; we need to keep our employees safe and happy; we need to be able to reinvest in new and improved products, markets, facilities, and equipment; and we need to make good profits. But how can you tell if a business is successful? Obviously it is difficult, if not impossible, to measure some of the objectives in direct financial terms — for example how do you measure whether your employees are happy? But there are many individuals and groups interested in, and in some cases dependent on, the company's performance, both inside and outside the company. Each interested party requires information relating to their own particular concern. For this reason, the company annual report and accounts document no longer merely reflects financial results but also contains a great deal of general information. It is a good way of finding out a lot about a company quickly and easily. If you are new to a company or about to join a company it is worth looking at the annual reports and accounts for the last two years to see how that company has performed; whom it owns and who owns part of it; to whom it owes money or by whom it is owed money.

To enable the company to produce the financial information, accounts must be kept during the course of business. This is done by cost accounting. The role of cost accounting is to identify the basic control factors used in managing a business. A key factor in running a business is delegating responsibility, but for delegation to work there should be a control system for checking performance. A cost accounts system provides such a facility. The need for cost accounting develops with the size of the company. Obviously in a small business the owner or manager can usually judge, using common sense or intuition, the state of the business. As a business grows, top management invariably becomes remote from the factory floor, authority is delegated and a control system is needed to measure performance.

Cost accounts (or the elements of cost accounts such as standard costs, cost centres, etc.) are the facets of accounting with which non-financial managers most commonly come into contact because, in a well run company, the cost accounting structure permeates the whole business and thereby allows management to keep track of day-to-day activities.

The flows of money into and out of a business are shown by two main documents, the main financial records, which are the profit

Example of a balance sheet

```
        Balance sheet of J & J Manufacturing Ltd
                as at 31 December 1988
```

	£		£
Share capital	200	Fixed Assets:	
		— Land & Buildings	75
		— Plant & Machinery	85
Reserves	50	— Office Equipment	20
		— Motor Vehicles	30
			210
Long-term loans	160		
		Current Assets:	
		— Stocks	200
		— Debtors	120
		— Cash	5
			325
		LESS:	
		Current liabilities	
		— Creditors	(120)
		— Bank overdraft	(20)
			(140)
		Net current assets	**185**
		Investments	15
	410		410

and loss account and the balance sheet. These are both terms with which most people are familiar but which many would find it hard to explain.

A balance sheet is a picture of the company taken at a particular moment in time — a kind of snapshot, freezing the company's financial situation at any one moment. It is a measure of the wealth of the company at that moment which, when compared with an earlier balance sheet, could be used to assess the growth of the company in the intervening period.

Why is it called a balance sheet? It is called that because the assets, liabilities, and capital of the company will all balance at any one time — the total of the debits must balance the total of credits. On page 118 is an example of a simple balance sheet, and notice that the time at which it is prepared is always given.

Many financial experts rate the balance sheet as the more important document, with the profit and loss account merely adding information to supplement that provided by the balance sheet. The profit and loss budget records all the income from sales or services and deducts all costs, direct costs such as labour, materials, and production overheads, and indirect costs such as sales and marketing distribution, administration, research and development. This then leaves a profit, or loss, but does not give as much detailed information as other financial statements.

Cash management is very important to keep a business running. In a company cash means actual cash, money in the bank, and short term investments which can be easily converted into cash. Cash (or treasury) management is important for three main reasons:

- It is necessary for a company to meet everyday payments in the normal course of business to employees, creditors, the tax man etc., as well as to pay for purchases of fixed assets.
- It provides a buffer against unexpected cash needs.
- It will enable the company to take advantage of 'bargains'; for example, a company involved in the purchase of commodity raw materials, such as copper for electrical components, may well take advantage of a price fall to purchase

large stocks. Similarly any company which is involved in international trading needs to manage its foreign currency cash flows well in order to take advantage of favourable currency movements.

Although a company needs to hold cash it must be able to earn profit through longer term investments where the interest or return is greater.

Cash flow is vitally important to small businesses who may not have the longer term investment to fall back on. Small companies have gone out of business when they were in fact profitable because their cash flow was negative. This arises when they are dealing with suppliers who need quick payment and customers or clients who take a long time to pay them. This means that to get a job done they have to pay out to suppliers but have to wait a long time before they get payment from their customers, thus having to run into an overdraft situation which costs them money.

Most of the arithmetic in the main financial statements is simple addition or subtraction so once you learn to look at them as simple lists of what the company has acquired or spent they will not seem so daunting.

Business and computing jargon

Other areas of business also have their own specialist jargon, for example computing and information technology, but business itself also has specialist terms. Some of this are given below:

ASAP	As soon as possible.
BCC	Blind copy to (i.e. do not list this person in the 'copies to' list).
CC	Copy to.
CFI	Copy for information (i.e. no action required).
GIGO	Garbage in – garbage out (originally a computer term but now often used for people).

Key skills for success in business

KISS	Keep it simple, stupid, keep it short and simple, OR keep it simple and succinct.
LIFO	Last in first out (usually used when speaking about redundancies).
MODUS OPERANDI	(Latin) Way of working (e.g. peculiar to this person).
TBA	To be advised.

Computing is the other area where jargon and acronyms are rife. Names and terms are bandied about and because everyone else seems to know what they mean we are often loath to ask. Below are listed some of the more common but less obvious ones:

BOOT UP	Start up the computer or computer system. This is a set procedure you have to go through to start the system running.
BUG	An error in the computer software.
CAD	Computer aided design; usually applied to electronic drafting systems where single shapes can be manipulated independently.
CADCAM	Computer aided design — Computer aided manufacturing.
CIM	Computer integrated manufacturing.
COMMS LINKS	This is short for 'communication links' and applies to the links between different parts of the computer system. These can be local or over great distances.
CPI	Characters per inch or the number of letters, symbols or numbers which a printer can print into a horizontal line one inch long.

CPS	This relates to printers and means 'characters per second' i.e. the number of characters produced by the printer in one second.
CPU	The central processing unit or 'brains' of the computer.
CRASH	The breakdown in the computer system, usually caused by an error in the software.
DEFAULT	A value assigned by the program or printer when no other value is supplied.
DEBUG	To sort out an error in computer software.
DISK	A device for holding information for a computer, it can either be a 'hard disk' permanently installed in the computer system or smaller 'floppy disks' which are put in by the user.
DOWN LOADING	Sending data from the computer's central processor to another device or another part of the system.
DP	Short for data processing or handling and manipulating of data on the computer.
DTP	Desk top publishing — a phrase coined by Paul Brainerd of Aldus to imply that that much of the role of the traditional typesetter and printer can be emulated by low cost desk top computers.
HARDWARE	All the physical equipment that makes up a computer system. Any part of the computer system which is solid and you can touch is hardware.
ICON	A small graphic symbol which visually represents the meaning of a command on the computer screen.

LOG ON	To 'sign on' or go through a procedure to identify yourself and gain access to the program.
LOG OFF	The user exit procedure, that is to tell the computer that you have finished and 'sign off'.
PC	Personal computer — a micro-computer which is used by only one user at a time.
MEMORY	The storage in the computer system; it stores data and programs while processing is being carried out and is a device from which data can be retrieved.
MOUSE	A small hand-held device whose movement across the desk produces corresponding movement of a pointer across the computer screen. It is used as a way of giving instructions to a computer.
NETWORK	Computers and peripherals linked together by a data transmission system (for example a telephone line).
PROGRAM	A set of coded instructions for a computer system to follow.
RAM	Random access memory — electronic memory which allows access to the data stored there and will allow you to change or add to it. Data in RAM is lost when the machine is switched off.
REAL TIME	When you put information into the computer the database is actually changed to include that information there or then if it is working in real time. So, every time the computer is used the information is updated and any data you ask for will include all the latest details available.

ROM	Read Only Memory — this only allows the computer to 'read' the information which is stored there. It cannot be altered and is kept in the computer when it is switched off.
SOFTWARE	The program that instructs the computer system.
VDU	Visual Display Unit — the part of the computer which looks like a television screen and displays the information for you to read.
WINDOW	One section of the computer's display screen which can be treated independently from the rest of the screen to scroll data, show graphics, or present a menu.
WP	Word Processing — sophisticated 'typing' system which will enable you to type documents onto the computer and which will automatically cope with tasks such as carriage returns and page breaks. It will also allow you to move individual words or blocks of text around the screen, alter spellings and other information before you print it out.
WYSIWYG	What you see is what you get — this means that what you see on the screen is what you will actually get printed out on the paper.

Meetings

There are various types of meetings, ones where you go out to meet one or two individuals at their own premises or mutually convenient venue; one-to-one meetings at your own company, for example between you and your boss or you and a subordinate;

meetings of several people called by someone else, and meetings of several people which you have called and therefore can control.

Although many factors are common to all these meetings, to make the best use of each of these situations they do need to be treated differently. Women are very good communicators and there are certain types of work where this is especially important, but there are other areas where communication appears less obvious but is just as vital to doing the job. Good communication skills pervade all walks of life and all types of work, women should capitalize on the natural ability they have in this area. Meetings are an opportunity for you to do this.

When meeting other people being a woman is sometimes helpful; as well as getting you noticed it means that people will remember you and know who you are. When joining a new company this could be a disadvantage because they will get to know you before you get to know them, so you may have to make an effort to learn names and faces very quickly. When you go out from your company to other companies as an ambassador this ability to be noticed can be very useful, and is one you should not shy away from or be ashamed of.

Advantages women managers have

- Because women in management positions are still unusual men do remember more readily the women they have met at meetings, and if you telephone somebody for an appointment afterwards they may be likely to talk to you because they remember you.

- Being a woman and being attractive can help to get you an appointment, but having got in to see somebody you *must* then be able to deliver.

- Because women need to be liked, they frequently also like other people and enjoy talking to them. This may enable you to get people to talk to you, and may also encourage them to talk because they enjoy your company. This in itself is a skill and should not be underrated.

Meetings one-to-one

These situations can give you a good grounding for handling people in large groups by developing your confidence and knowledge of your subject. In whatever situation you must learn to **get your message across:** the keys to this are:

1. *Do your homework*: know what you want, why you want it and know what the other person knows as well.

2. *Analyse your audience*: if it is an individual, what type is he — play to his type. If it is a group, focus to the group personality or identify the opinion leaders and analyse them.

3. *Plan and rehearse*: think positively about yourself giving the presentation or talking to that individual and doing it successfully.

4. *Control*: maintain emotional control.

5. *State your point*: clearly and directly, don't over-explain, hedge, or put riders to it.

6. *Think of a benefit*: what benefit is there to the listener? Explain what is in it for them.

7. *Keep it simple*: make your point then stop talking. Often the less you say the more impact you make.

Group meetings

Meetings in larger groups, apart from having more people, also have the added complication of politics. Men seem to think that meetings are essential, they are important for finding out how to defeat rivals, the latest office politics and so on. Comparative research into men and women in management has shown that meetings show up a lot of differences. At the end of meetings women tend to have reached agreement. The men can be very sharp with each other and the real meeting takes place afterwards. In the average business meeting with either all men or mostly men the people present give verbal agreement but in actual fact often don't agree in their hearts. This means that they will walk away from the meeting without really agreeing and are quite likely to undermine the decisions without trying to make them work. This means that the meeting hasn't really achieved its objective of making progress towards an idea. Women will use a different style which takes account of everyone's position and tries to move the whole group ahead. It can be very effective and is in fact the method used by the Japanese. The Japanese have a management style in which the whole group agrees, because by the time they get to a meeting they have all been approached in advance and the meeting is a formality.

Before the meeting, whether you or somebody else is organizing it, it is important that you are prepared. If someone else has called the meeting make sure that you know why the meeting is being held and if there is no agenda ask for one. You should also find out why you are needed at the meeting. Make a note of the date, time, and place of the meeting and ensure that you allow yourself enough time to get them. Study the agenda and start to think about the items which will be discussed. If you think there are other topics which should be included, let the Chairman know in good time; if you want to raise an important issue, dealing with it under 'any other business' is unfair to everyone concerned, not least to yourself. Read any material which has been circulated with the agenda and check your facts then ask any questions you need to beforehand. If you want other people present to read papers to back up your points, send them to the Chairman before the meeting, but avoid lengthy papers.

When you are involved in a meeting and you want to contribute you must make sure you are heard and that your contribution is valuable. The rules described earlier in this section for **getting your message across** are just as important in a group meeting. But in addition you must remember the following points:

1. *Let others have their say*: if you disagree be tactful, courteous, and patient.

2. *If you don't understand something, don't be afraid to ask for clarification.* Others will probably be in the same boat and be grateful for the chance to get it cleared up.

3. *Be constructive not destructive*: putting another person's idea down may mean that he keeps his next idea to himself and you could lose a good idea.

4. *Make your own notes.* They usually aid concentration and you may wish to record your impressions of other views and reactions.

5. *When you do volunteer your opinion choose the best time to do it*: if you speak at the beginning or the end your ideas will be remembered and you will appear more persuasive. Avoid the mass of discussion in the middle of the meeting wherever possible.

6. *Do not belittle your contribution* by prefacing your statement with words that diminish you such as 'may be' or 'possibly'. Make statements rather than ask questions: do not apologize for your views by making statements like 'I'm sorry but . . .' or 'excuse me, I was just . . .'. Try to avoid using 'um' and 'er': if you are well prepared this will help you to overcome these problems.

7. *When you are interrupted don't give way.* Turn and look at the person who is interrupting you, put your hand up in a stopping motion and say, 'John, excuse me, I wasn't finished', turn away and continue talking.

8. *If you are ignored, ask for a response to what you have just said* with a comment like, 'Before we move on to that point I would like the group's response to what I've just said'.

9. *If you are criticized, deal with it.* Ask the speaker to justify their comments. Don't always assume that criticism is bad, look for good in criticism — there may be good advice there and the criticism may be constructive. If you have made a mistake, admit it is true and move on. If there is a problem, attempt to solve it but don't be drawn into an argument in front of the group. State your opinion unemotionally, and if someone else is getting emotional don't get caught up in this: make a comment like 'I do not

think it is appropriate to discuss this here or now' and look at the Chairman to enlist his or her help. Finally, know when to discount the criticism.

Holding a meeting

When you are in a position of calling a meeting you need to be in control of that meeting. It also puts upon you certain responsibilities for preparation and planning. The following key points should be borne in mind.

1. Ask yourself 'do I really need this meeting?' If you do not need a meeting don't hold it: 'we always have a departmental meeting every Monday morning' is not a good enough reason to take up people's valuable time.

2. Decide on your objective and keep it clearly in mind at all stages.

3. Plan the meeting carefully, decide who is to be present (ensure that all and only the people necessary are present) circulate the agenda and any relevant information well in advance.

4. Plan and book the venue and equipment and prepare your visual aids well in advance, checking them just before the meeting.

5. Plan the time for the meeting carefully: certain parts of the week or day may not be as productive as others for a variety of reasons. If you anticipate a short meeting, start at a time that will encourage a prompt ending — for example an hour before lunch or towards the end of the working day. If you anticipate a long meeting, remember that few people can keep their concentration satisfactorily after about two hours. If it is likely to be long then plan a break during the meeting. Agree time limits in advance and start on time. Don't penalize those who have come on time by waiting for those who are late. Plan the agenda carefully, allocating specific amounts of time to each item but including time to establish the aims of the meeting, ensure effective discussion,

reach conclusions, and agree the actions necessary.

6. Ensure, when minutes are necessary, that someone else takes them *not you*, that they are concise and definite, and include reference to who is to do what and by when.

7. Remember that as Chairman you must act both as leader and referee. Make sure you arrive in plenty of time yourself and start promptly. If outsiders are present introduce them and explain why they are there.

8. Sit so that you can be seen by everyone and you can also see anyone who wishes to contribute. Control the talkative, some people like to speak just to hear themselves talk and others take a long time to say a little. Make sure you bring in the silent — new or junior people could be reluctant speakers, encourage them to contribute their views.

9. End meetings on a positive note, summarize decisions taken, actions to be implemented and persons responsible. Be polite, thank everyone for participating, and if appropriate fix the date and time and place for next meeting. Finish on time, don't let the meeting drag on.

It is worthwhile analysing your performance as Chairman regularly, and being prepared to solicit feedback so that you can develop your skills. Ask colleagues for feedback on your meetings but be sure that you ask in a positive way, for example 'how did you feel about the length of the meeting on such and such a date?' instead of 'that meeting last Monday dragged on, didn't it?' And be sure to listen and take note of what they say.

Managing paperwork

Receiving written communications

Written communication is two-way, so as well as sending out memos, letters, and reports, you will receive a lot of information in writing. Dealing with this can be very time consuming and learning to do it efficiently can be a great bonus. Follow the rules below and it will help you a great deal.

1. Avoid clutter. When you are working on anything, clear your desk of all paper except the specific job in hand. Your desk is not a receptacle for 'things to do'. Keep letter trays for this.

2. Make sure your work space is organized so that things you need are close to hand. Having to get up and walk to get something is only an excuse for breaking your train of concentration.

3. Eliminate unnecessary paperwork, and simplify paperwork wherever possible. For example, don't ask for reports if you don't really need them.

4. Handle each piece of paper only once. Discipline yourself to make a decision on every piece of paper that crosses your desk, there and then, even if it is only a decision to seek advice or decide when to review it again, then put it straight into its correct place.

5. When you get a memo that requires only a brief reply, write the reply onto that memo, photocopy it for your reference and send the original back. If it needs a typed reply, again write notes on the original letter and give it to your secretary to compose and type the reply letter.

6. Do not communicate on paper when you want to get candid opinions or are seeking sensitive information. Use paperwork for facts, to confirm or clarify.

7. Sort paperwork into categories in priority order:
(1) important or urgent;
(2) important but not urgent;
(3) urgent but not important;
(4) not urgent or important.

Some of the category (3)s may need to be done before category (1)s. Use your letter trays for today, tomorrow, and awaiting reply, or set up a 'bring forward' system which will automatically bring papers to mind on the correct date.

8. Keep a file for paperwork that you can leave alone unless someone asks for it — a 'slush file'. Don't keep anything you won't need; the bin is a useful tool. Ask yourself 'do I really *need* this on file?'

9. When reading, learn to identify quickly the key points in letters and reports; highlight these and make notes for action as you go through.

10. Distinguish between material that should be read carefully and that which can be skimmed.

11. If you have a lot of trade journals and articles to read to keep up to date, share it with colleagues. Each take one journal, go through it and highlight only the areas worth reading or points to note and swap within the agreed timescale.

Writing memos, letters and reports

When it comes to you producing reports, letters, and memos, remember that those who will read them are as busy as you. If you can help them by being clear, succinct, and worthwhile they are more likely to read your work and act on it.

Business situations are likely to include a great variety of communications for a variety of purposes. Each of us has a personal writing style; there is nothing wrong with this, but for business communication you should develop a style which is simple and straightforward.

Always get letters and reports typed: memos and compliment slips are acceptable in handwriting, blue or black ink. Whatever you are writing make sure you are clear, concise, and accurate. Before you begin, assemble all the information, including any relevant figures and references. For all but the shortest letters or memos make a list of points and sort them into a logical sequence. This will help you when dictating or writing out in longhand and save several attempts at drafting. The advent of word processing has made many of us lazy at this but it is always worthwhile and a good discipline to get into. There may be occasions when you have to produce a report without access to word processing, and then your good habits will be invaluable.

For letters and memos there may be a standard layout and style used in your company, check to see if there is and if so what it is. A senior secretary or member of the corporate identify department may be able to furnish you with a standardized layout document. It is important that written communications, even a hand written memo, are well presented, as bad presentation can detract from your message.

Memos

The memo is one of the most useful ways of communicating within a company.

In memos do not put in extraneous language — use bullet points, headings, and brief phrases. Who is going to read a six page memo? Keep it short and simple (KISS) and get to the point. Think in outlines and subheadings. Always be sure your recipient knows exactly what you want without having to wade through reams of unnecessary padding.

If there is no standard form invent your own system and stick to it. Every memo should include:

- Name and title of recipient.
- His or her department.
- Your name and title.
- Your department. (Even if you know him or her well, he may wish to show it to someone who doesn't know you.)
- Date.
- Subject.

The wording can be less formal than a letter, depending on your style, but keep it brief and to the point. The two examples below

XYZ Manufacuturing company

INTERNAL MEMO

TO: John Brown
Manager, Training

FROM: Jane Young
Manager, Marketing

DATE: 20:7:89

SUBJECT: SALES TRAINING COURSE

Your memo of 17:7:89 received, and change of timings noted. Yes, this is acceptable. Go ahead and print the programme.

Jane Young
Jane Young

Example A: Memo pro-forma with typed reply.

XYZ Manufacturing company

FAO — JOHN BROWN
MANAGER, TRAINING

FROM — JANE YOUNG
MANAGER, MARKETING

John,

RE: SALES TRAINING COURSE

Thanks for your memo of last Monday. I'm quite happy with the changes to schedule you suggest, please go ahead and print the programme.

Jane
20th July 89

Example B: Blank memo with handwritten reply.

show a memo on a standard form and another on paper with just a heading; they are different replies to the same memo.

Letters

In writing business letters the same basic rules apply, but you should write in whole sentences within the body of the letter (unless making bullet points or lists) and always have it typed.

There are many good books on business letter writing, including standard formats for specific needs, so if you need more help read some of these.

If you are fairly confident, it is worth looking at some letters from top secretaries in your company to see how they are presented. If you have your own secretary, she should know how to present a business letter, but if she is new to the company get a copy of the company's layout from your corporate identity department for her to follow. It's no good shouting at her for producing something that is wrong unless you ensure that she knows what is wanted in the first place.

Reports

Reports are a much larger and more complex undertaking than letters or memos. A 'report' can be defined as 'a document in which a given problem is examined for the purpose of conveying information, reporting findings, putting forward ideas, and sometimes, making recommendations.'

Again there are books and courses on this subject and don't be afraid to ask your secretary (if you have one) or an experienced colleague to help advise you on layout.

If you remember the ABC of writing — ACCURATE, BRIEF and CLEAR — and follow the twenty steps which follow, you will be well on the way to producing reports that have impact.

There are three main stages in producing a report: Before you begin; Writing the report; Review and revise your report.

Before you begin:

- What? Find out exactly what you have been asked to do, and get concise terms of reference.
- Why? Find out why you have been asked to write this report and establish clearly in your mind the subject, scope, and purpose of the report (is it to give information, report findings, put forward ideas, or recommend a course of action?)
- Who? Who is your reader and what does he or she want to know?
- What does the reader already know?
- What type of jargon or terminology will the reader be able to understand?
- How is this report to be used?
- Marshal all your facts. Collect facts and ideas about your subject and have to hand any references or further information you may need. They can be jotted down as notes and outlines of ideas at this stage.
- Check your facts for accuracy. A whole report can be damned if a reader finds something which he knows is inaccurate.
- List the key headings and sort them into a logical order. This is your framework on which the report will be built.

Now you are ready to begin to write the actual report.

Writing the report:

- Write down the purpose of your report in one simple sentence. Whenever you are unsure of whether or not to include a point look back at this sentence and see if it fits in with your task. When you have written your purpose down, choose a title. Keep it simple and brief and use it to reflect your purpose for the reader.
- In the light of your purpose and title consider your collective facts and ideas. Reject any which are not helpful to your case

or necessary to your purpose, and make a note of any additional information you may now decide that you need.

- Look back at your list of headings: consider them carefully and critically. If necessary revise them or alter the groupings.

- Look back at the order in which you have planned to present your information and again revise this critically. Give each section heading a title and number so that you can easily refer to it in any discussion in the report.

- Fill in each subject area. You can now arrange your material within the divisions, arranging the material in an order which is easy for the readers to follow, clear and succinct.

- Draw conclusions and make recommendations. Decide whether to group these in a section on their own or at the end of each division in the report (see note, page 138, on the executive summary). Make sure that your conclusions or recommendations are in line with the facts that you have presented.

- Consider whether you want to use illustrations to supplement or replace parts of your text.

Now that you have the first draft of your report completed you should review it critically.

Reviewing the report:

- Look carefully at your title and subject headings. These titles should identify subject matter under them. They should be brief but three or four precise words which give information are better than one or two vague or ambiguous ones.

- Decide if you want to lift any factual details out of the main divisions and place them in appendices. This can help you to remove distracting detail and keep the main line of thought running through the report without interruption.

   At the same time you should consider whether you can reduce some long explanations to simple charts or diagrams or a list of bullet points and check whether your writing style is suitable for the target audience intended.

- Write an executive summary and put it at the beginning. If you put a conclusion at the end everyone will turn to that first anyway, so you might as well put it at the beginning! Keep this summary very concise with the key issues raised and main recommendations made — if at all possible keep it to one side of A4. If your reader is interested he or she will read on to find the detail.

- Check the presentation. Get it properly laid out with a title page which contains:
  - Date
  - Title/Subject
  - Author
  - Intended Target Audience

  If the report is longer than a few pages, follow the title page with a contents page. At the end of the report list any references used or further reading suggested.

It is always useful to get a colleague to read what you have written. They are not as close to it as you and may be able to make helpful suggestions about clarifying points or improving your writing style. Sharing experience in this way will help you to learn and improve.

Making presentations and speaking in public

One of the biggest worries for many people in business, both men and women, is speaking in public. Men are less likely to admit their fears and when asked they will say 'yes', whereas women, being less sure of themselves, will often turn down an opportunity. This is a great pity because not only are you passing over a chance to get yourself noticed and state your case, but you are likely to be much better at it than your male colleagues are.

Key skills

Having watched Liz Clarke give a presentation to a group of training officers it is obvious to me that she 'sells' herself and her ideas well; this is largely due to her experience in retailing, but is partly a personal trait. This enables her to persuade people to listen to what she is saying. She is good at diagnosing what the customer wants, again based on experience, but feels she is more understanding than male colleagues and likes to bring everyone along with her by her influence and persuasion rather than direction. She can, however, be tough with a group she is training if she needs to be. Working in a training environment there are certain areas where she has to overcome suspicion or distrust right at the start, because of being a woman. Liz sets out six steps to this:

- Establish credibility — who I am and what I've done. Be brief.

- Set a supportive but businesslike climate and if you can do it well, introduce some humour.

- Make sure your presentation has logical structure and set out the objectives clearly. Ask what delegates want from the seminar.

- Treat everyone with respect (even if you have to confront).

- Ask for feedback and give your group what they are looking for.

- Make the last two minutes memorable.

She feels that women are better prepared when giving presentations and generally are very good presenters. But she still accepts that women have to be a bit better than the men to do well and are not supported by all male groups as much as her male colleagues would be. As a woman speaker people often think that you will not have much to offer them but you must give them something positive quickly and show you are professional. Establishing your credibility through what you know is always a good starting point.

Another one of the people I talked to who has a lot of experience at giving presentations is Christina Gearing. She feels that in some jobs being a woman is a positive advantage, especially where you have to deal with people outside your company. For example, in her job as Account Director for the International Convention Centre, Christina has to give presentations and talk to people all over the world; she talks about the advantages of the new Convention Centre and how it can help other organizations with their meetings and conferences.

She still feels that a woman in her position is unusual enough to be noticed and therefore people will remember her. She also takes great pleasure in people's surprise at her professionalism and positive approach. She feels that women try that bit harder and therefore have high standard and are very professional. Any woman who regularly gives presentations has worked hard at it and prepared well; consequently, because she puts so much into it, her presentation is usually accurate and has flair and style, while many male colleagues take it as routine and will only give a mediocre presentation. Christina feels that the natural need of women to be appreciated may account for some of this extra effort which makes us strive to achieve acceptance: it also makes us quick to criticize ourselves and analyse our performances to enable us to improve in the future. In all aspects of our work we ask a lot of ourselves and expect to have to be better, but we are willing to and want to learn especially from those around us. This puts us in a good position to develop and grow.

Having agreed to give a presentation, how do you go about it? First of all you must know what you have let yourself in for. When you agree to give the presentation, ask the following ten questions:

1. What are the objectives and why am I doing this?

2. Who is it for and what is their background?

3. How many will there be in the audience?

4. Will I be alone or will there be others before or after me?

5. If there are others, who are they, and what is the order of presentation?
6. How much time will I have?
7. Do you want time left for questions at the end?
8. What visual aids equipment can be provided?
9. What is the venue?
10. What is the date and time?

Keep this as a check-list and make sure you ask these questions on every single occasion. When you have this information you can then prepare. Giving effective presentations is an important skill to develop for your career. It is quite normal to be nervous, but you can learn to overcome this by careful preparation, which will give you the confidence to know that you are talking about your subject well, and practise. Use the following twelve tips to develop your presentation skills:

1. Be prepared. Write out your speech, think it through, find real interest and excitement in it, and then practise it. Practise giving your speech in front of a mirror with a tape recorder, with a video recorder, or even better to a sympathetic colleague or friend.

2. Don't read out your speech word for word but use cue cards, index cards, or a highlighted outline, for reference if you lose your train of thought. The security of having these notes is the best reason for having them available — you may not even need to use them.

3. Arrive at the venue early and allow yourself time to get settled. If it is some distance away and you are giving your presentation early in the morning it is even worthwhile travelling down the night before and stopping over to ensure you don't arrive flustered and late because you got caught in a traffic jam.

4. When you are introduced take a deep breath and begin by thanking your introducer and the audience. Look con-

fident and relaxed, your voice will reflect this. Remember that the audience wants you to be successful; they have come to hear what you have to say.

5. Make the opening positive, do something within the first five minutes to get the audience to participate. Ask them a direct question, use humour, get them talking to each other or challenge them with a statistic or fact that affects them directly.

6. Be aware that along with the words, you are sending your audience the feeling and emotion of your message.

7. Use words which the audience will understand — avoid jargon. Keep the message short and simple, make your points clearly and directly.

8. Use examples. People can relate to stories, examples, and analogies, and they also remember them more easily and for longer than facts and numbers. Make the stories amusing if you can, but do not tell set-piece jokes.

9. Use visuals as often as possible to hold the attention of the audience. Make sure the visuals are appropriate for your group and the size of the room. Only put up key points, not pages of close type, or use pictorial illustrations or simple charts and diagrams. Remember you want your visuals to reinforce your message, not detract from what you are saying.

10. Be prepared for any criticism or arguments and have an answer ready. Remember our notes on meetings earlier in this chapter.

11. End your question and answer time before the questions end. This means the audience will still be thinking about the presentation when you have finished.

12. Be enthusiastic — you have got something important to say, so enjoy it.

It may take a little while before you can really relax and enjoy giving presentations but it can be such an asset to your career that it is worth working at it and getting it right.

You do have the skills

As I said at the beginning of this chapter, women have a lot of good business skills, although we tend to underrate ourselves. By building on the skills we have, learning new techniques, and adding to our skills, we have the ability to achieve and succeed. Learn the techniques, practise and use them.

Taking positions in societies and voluntary organizations is a good training ground for business. You will learn to organize things, work together in groups, conduct meetings, and make decisions. Organizations such as Junior Chamber are a very good training ground as well.

Women as managers

In managing people women analyse and support their employees much better than men. They are often more subtle and caring, having learnt from experience of a different sort of life to that of their male colleagues.

Women managers generally have good interpersonal skills because they are prepared to listen and spend the time with people to make sure that they are well prepared and well motivated. However, although women have a need to be liked, men seem to think that this doesn't matter so long as they are respected; to a male manager it matters less what people think as long as they are performing well. This leads to the question, 'What is a good manager?' If somebody ensures that his department delivers on time and to budget, then that measure of performance usually leads to the conclusion that he or she is a good manager. However, the way that this performance is achieved may not be ideal, for example a lot of male managers have poor interpersonal skills and their teams may be motivated more by fear of failure than wishing to do the task for the manager concerned. Women can achieve and build good team relationships if they want to.

Partly because of their need to be liked, women find disciplining people distasteful. However, when they do confront the issue they may be more constructive and considerate in their criticism. This reticence to discipline people may mean that a woman manager would cover up for people who are not competent or performing well whereas a man would expose them quicker. You must remember that your performance will be judged by the performance of your team, and you cannot afford to carry members who are not pulling their weight. It may be a case of a need for training or support, but if it is a problem it should be sorted out and not allowed to continue.

Have the courage to do what you need to — you have the basic ability and you can acquire the skills.

Chapter Seven

Becoming powerful

Being assertive

When women put themselves down they often elevate others. We criticize ourselves, idealize others, see ourselves as weak and those in authority as powerful and strong. But this view of authority is unrealistic and it means that it is hard for us to have the productive team relationships with higher level people which are necessary for moving ahead. It also means that we often fail to take initiatives in the workplace and tend to see ourselves as reporters, not solvers, of problems. We need to learn to rely on ourselves more — however, you cannot build confidence overnight. Being confident is part of your own self-image but you can be helped to seem confident by being assertive.

Before you can become powerful you must learn to be assertive. Being assertive is not the same as being aggressive, you must stand up for your rights while accepting that other people also have rights.

When we are assertive we tell people what we want or need or prefer. We make our statement clearly and confidently, do not belittle ourselves or others and do not behave in a threatening way or put down other people. Being assertive is a positive way of behaving but does not involve denying the rights of other people on the way.

Agressive behaviour threatens, punishes, or puts down other people. An aggressive person intends to get their own way no matter what. We behave aggressively when we are sarcastic, manipulative, spread gossip or are racist or sexist. By using these tactics we can get our own way but it probably leaves someone else with bad feelings. Behaving aggressively may get you what you want in the short-term but it can also store up trouble for future dealings with that person. Aggressive people often stand too close to others, stand when others sit, point or wag their fingers, and use loud tones of voice. They may touch and pat other people (for example on the arm or shoulder) which is patronizing and reduces the status of the other person.

At the other end of the scale are passive people who are often low on self-confidence and self-esteem. They may even feel that they are so unimportant that their own needs are not valuable and that they do not deserve the help or attention of others. Passive people tend to leave everything to fate or chance and hope they will get what they want by expecting others to guess their wishes. As a result of this they often end up feeling angry with others when those people did not know what they wanted. Passive people often have a hesitant stance with their head bowed or held to one side. They may shift from one foot to the other and not look people in the eye; they are also likely to preface statements with 'um', 'er', 'I'm sorry', cough nervously, or look embarrassed.

Passive behaviour is powerless and aggressive behaviour is overpowering. *Assertive behaviour is powerful.* Traditional upbringing has led women to expect to be submissive, i.e. passive and powerless. In an attempt to overcome this we have frequently gone too far and adopted aggressive behaviour. But it is the middle ground of assertiveness which will help us to achieve our ends effectively.

If we are able to express our feelings constructively and be open with others about what we want, we are more likely to get the kind of relationships we want, the job we want, the friends we want, the society we want, and the life we want. Assertive people are more confident, less frustrated, less anxious, and less likely to upset others.

Assertiveness skills

Assertive behaviour is a positive process and these are the key skills which you need to master.

1. *Know what you want.* To be able to appear confident you need to be sure of what you want; don't ask for something that you may eventually realize is not what you want.

2. *Say what you want.* Come straight out with it, don't hesitate or beat about the bush. If you are worried, practise before you say it. And say it at the right time, don't let too much time pass as this builds up worry; on the other hand don't say it when you are emotional or angry.

3. *Be specific.* Say exactly what you do or do not want so there cannot be any misunderstanding. You do not need a long explanation or justification for what you have to say.

4. *Use eye contact.* Look directly at the person — if you cannot look them in the eye you will look shifty and you will not come across as someone who knows what they want.

5. *Be relaxed.* If you are shifting from one foot to the other or waving your arms around or being so still and stiff that it is unnatural, you will show the other person that you are anxious. It is even worth practising looking relaxed in a mirror.

6. *Use an even tone of voice.* Don't whine and avoid laughing nervously. If you giggle or laugh you won't look as if you mean what you say, and a whining tone is only irritating to the listener.

7. *Neither plead nor be sarcastic — be direct and honest.* Pleading can either annoy the person or make them feel guilty, in which case you are being manipulative. Being sarcastic communicates hostility as you put the other person down.

Putting your assertiveness skills to the test

Refusing a request

It is easier to put these skills into practice when you are in control — you can plan, practise and choose your moment — but sometimes it is not under your control and when you are approached by someone else you may have to adapt these points slightly. If someone asks you to do something you don't want to do, how do you handle it? Consider this example:

Malcolm: 'I've just got to get these in the post tonight, could you help me out and type them up for me?'

Jane: 'I'm busy myself at present.'

Malcolm: 'Oh surely you can put something aside just to do this for half an hour?'

Jane: 'No, I need to get this done now.'

Malcolm: 'I thought you'd be able to help out a pal.'

Jane: 'I would help if I could, but I need to get this done now.'

A couple of minutes later Malcolm goes away and gets on with his own work.

He gave up but did not go away angry because Jane had been firm but polite. She had ignored his assumption that her work was less important than his and the hidden implication that she was being selfish, and so was not tricked into explaining her reasons or defending herself. She kept to the point and was persistent. This tactic can also be useful in a meeting when red herrings are constantly raised. Be persistent and it can bring the meeting back to the subject you want.

Dealing with 'put downs'

One weapon used by aggressive people is the 'put down' or 'side swipe'. For example, in our example above Malcolm says 'I thought you'd be able to help out a pal'. Jane could have retaliated but chose to ignore it and stick to the point at issue.

Put downs include phrases like:

- 1 'I can't find anything in this bookcase — you women always have such weird ways of storing things — I don't understand how you can work like this.'

- 2 'Oh women are all the same.'
- 3 'Don't be a spoil sport.'
- 4 'I know it will be hard for you, because you like to have your own way.'

In each case it would be easy to react angrily — this will only play into the hands of your critic. If you cannot ignore the comment then you need to reply in a way that will not seem defensive or angry, and will not put the other person down — there is no point in turning it into a slanging match or making you an enemy.

Can you think of an assertive response to each of the statements?

1. The first may have some truth in it, but has been exaggerated. You should respond to the truth and ignore the rest:

    'They are all filed alphabetically under author from the top left shelf.'

This response is called *fogging*. It accepts and answers the truth but ignores the other comments.

2. (+4.) The second and last questions can be answered by *negative enquiry*. That is actively seeking specific criticism.

    'In what ways are we all the same?'

    'What makes you say I always want my own way?'

If the critic is genuine he can give you some useful feedback which you can act on; if not then your question will be fobbed off with answers such as 'Oh, it's just an expression' or 'I didn't mean it'.

3. The third comment could be dealt with by a simple statement:

    'But that is not *my* idea of sport.'

4. And the last comment could be countered with:

'But you're not me' or 'How do you know that?'

Don't preface your answers with phrases such as 'I'm sorry' or 'I'm afraid', this will diminish what you say and make you seem passive.

Interruptions

Another problem with women which robs them of power is the fact that they are easily interruptible. They are interrupted more often than their male colleagues. There are three main techniques used by interrupters:

First, they may call your name out; this gets your attention.

Secondly, they will begin speaking at a faster rate than you were speaking.

Thirdly, they will speak at a higher volume than you were speaking.

You can parry the interruptions by using the same techniques: using the person's name, speaking at a faster pace, and speaking at a higher volume. However, if the interrupter is more senior to you this behaviour may seem too overpowering and you would do better to give way to their interruption at this time. You should, however, then be tenacious in coming back with your points at a later and more appropriate time, not too far away. Powerless people usually give up once they have been interrupted.

A way in which women make themselves more interruptible is that they do not put the point they are saying succinctly or forcefully enough, or they take too long a time to get to the point. Don't hedge and dance around the point. Doing this not only makes you more interruptible but also means that your points and comments do not come across with the force and conviction which they should. You should make the point you want to make quickly and succinctly. If you have done a lot of research to back up your comments you can always bring this in later in answer to questions or when enlarging on further comment. Spending time describing all your feelings, background, and research is a behaviour resulting from low self confidence. A male colleague will be much more confident and put his points more forcefully and directly. Having the confidence that the solution he has come up with is the correct one, he will present it in that way. Use the KISS system, keep it simple and succinct. That applies not only to written communication but also to oral communication.

Assertiveness and confidence

As well as what you say, how you say it and how you present yourself are important factors in being assertive. Remember the tips I gave earlier about self-image and presentation in Chapter Three? These are also part of being assertive. Believe in yourself and be confident — it will show through.

I would advise anybody who feels that they lack confidence to go on an assertiveness course. Liz Clarke has run many such courses and her clients come for a variety of reasons. For example:

- They feel they are not getting what they want in their lives or careers.
- They feel they are getting walked over.
- They feel they are being overlooked.
- They want to be heard and recognized.
- They want to take charge and take control of their direction in life.

Liz says that being assertive is about an 'I'm OK, you're OK' attitude, not the usual female approach of pleasing everybody all the time, and putting yourself second. It is a skill you can learn.

Assertiveness and others

We should also encourage younger people to take all the opportunities they can to build their confidence, for example joining in debates or role-play exercises. When they are working they must not neglect their development; encourage them to go on courses and get training and experience, share with others on the courses and learn from their experiences as well. If they can't go away on courses, help them to learn management skills from books or tapes and get to know people who can help them with advice and with whom they can talk and share experiences.

What is power?

Power is the ability to focus your energy towards an ultimate goal. Power is about control — control over yourself and control over others. Powerful people do not get side-tracked.

Powerful people show their power by the way they talk and how good they are at putting their case across. They show confidence. You cannot pussy-foot around with them, they expect a straight and an honest answer; when they ask questions they are searching and they are astute.

Professionalism brings power: intelligence is part of this but it is also a combination of experience, knowing what you are doing, confidence without being cocky, and assertiveness. Technical knowledge is also important, you must know your subject and be able to converse confidently with others about theirs.

Charisma is also part of power. What is it? It's the charm and personal magnetism that attracts people to you: it can hold people spellbound and is the highest form of personal power. However, personal power is only part of the power of a person within an organization. It is how you are able to exercise your power within that organization which determines how powerful you really are in that position.

The exercise of power involves person 'A' influencing person 'B' to do what 'A' wants. The reason why 'B' will do what 'A' wants will tell you what sort of power 'A' has in relation to 'B'. If 'B' complies but reluctantly or if 'B' complies willingly and closely with 'A's wishes, these factors will tell you how much power 'A' has in relation to 'B'.

The nature of influence and power within organizations is a complex subject and there has been much written on it. However, there is no blueprint for dealing effectively with power in work situations, since every situation presents a different set of circumstances within which people must try to influence each other.

Sources of power

Power can be based on a number of different types of resource:

1. *Formal Authority.* This gives you the right to make decisions and it is conferred upon you by higher management. It depends on other people's acceptance of your right to decide and is seldom sufficient on its own but is usually found in conjunction with one or more of the other types of power.

2. *Expertise.* This is specialist knowledge and skills which are usually acquired through professional training outside the organization. The more exclusive your expertise and the more useful it is seen to be in the organization, the more power you will have.

3. *Control of Resources.* This is the control of finance, information, or physical resources within the organization. People in relatively low league positions can have considerable control over resources, but the most power goes to those who control the most valued resources, particularly money and information.

4. *Interpersonal Skills.* This is the ability to persuade and to build good relationships. It can depend on your personal intuition and ability but also on acquired skills through training and practice.

Therefore we could say that sources of power are located either in your own knowledge and skills, or in your organizational context such as your place within the hierarchy which gives you authority, or a job which gives you control of resources. One type of power source may exist without the other but it is obviously an advantage to have both together. It could be said that power is a matter of opportunity; opportunity which you may or may not take, either intentionally or by default. It is very important that you do take opportunities to build and develop your skills and knowledge, and therefore are in a position to make better use of other opportunities such as your position in the organization, whenever these arise.

We have already mentioned that power is related to influence, and people's willingness to be influenced and to comply with the wishes of others very largely hinges on their perception of that person. For example, your expertise can only work for you as a source of power if the people you wish to influence see you as an expert. If they are not aware of the value of your expertise then it will not act as a powerful tool for you and you may have to demonstrate it by finding opportunities to show your expertise. Similarly if you wish to influence others by means of your authority you must consider whether your authority is credible to others. For example do they believe that higher management would back your decisions and support your right to make them?

Not only are people's perceptions of you able to affect your credibility and influence over them, but there is also the question of your own perception of your power. If you fail to make the most of your political opportunities because you are not aware of them then you will fail to exercise the power that is invested in you. Therefore you must try to obtain an actual picture of what you want, what others want, and what political opportunities both you and they have for achieving these aims, and you must make sure that the power that you have is seen as credible by others.

Who has power?

Looking around your organization at who gets what in terms of benefits can tell you a great deal about who the powerful are and about their values. Benefits can be psychological, such as a feeling of personal satisfaction, or they can be practical such as extra staff or equipment for a department. If you conform to the values of the powerful this can enhance your power, and teach you what you need to know, do or understand to move towards a similar position yourself. Development of your personal power can be divided into two main areas: strategic and personal. The strategic development of your power is your position within the organization and the ability to perform certain functions within it; your personal power development is to evolve personal tactics and skills which will enable you to appear powerful to others. But first you need to look at your position and examine your current sphere of influence.

Exercise — the power web

1. Take a piece of paper and in the centre draw a small box and write your name in it.

2. Around this list at random anyone who has an effect on your work (above or below you, in or outside the company).

3. Do they have the right to decide what you do? If so, draw a triangle round their name.

4. Do you have the right to decide what they do? If so, put a circle around their name.

5. Who depends on you for what? Draw a line between your name and theirs and if they depend on you put an arrow towards their name.

6. Upon whom do you depend, for what? Draw a line between their name and yours and if you depend on them draw an arrow towards you.

7. Where 3 and 6 coincide these people have real power over you. Stop and think about them, why do they have power? What do they have? Can you acquire it?

When you understand the nature of their power and yours, you will be in a better position to develop your own power and improve your situation.

Acquiring personal power skills

Many of the skills which we have looked at earlier in the book — communication skills, presentation skills, subject expertise, and so on — will enable you to improve your position and appear more powerful, but there are other additional skills which we should look at here.

Personal space

Each of us has around us an area which is our own personal space. If other people come too close or 'invade' that space we feel uncomfortable. Coming into somebody else's personal space is an overpowering behaviour and it is frequently used by men towards women — although it is not always intended to be overpowering. Our personal space extends about 12 to 18 inches around us, and in a professional situation it is over-familiar to come within that personal space. Those who do it do not usually do so to be over-intimate (although this is sometimes the intention) but because they have found that it gives them a feeling of power over the individual whose space they are invading. You need to have strategies for dealing with people who do this.

A normal reaction when someone comes too close is to back off and then talk rapidly to get the meeting or interview over with quickly. The first thing to do when someone stands too close is to realize what they are doing and the effect this is likely to have on you. When you have done that you must then make a positive decision about how you are going to react, not react in the way your natural instincts tell you. Firstly, you must stand your ground and not back off, then you must look at the individual and establish eye contact, finally you must talk at your normal speed and not try to rush through the discussion. Also the way you stand in these circumstances is important — if you are leaning backwards with your hands hanging limply at your side, you might as well have backed away. Stand upright and firm, and perhaps use your arms in a gesture that will reinforce your firmness — for example crossing your arms or even, in extreme cases, putting your hands on your hips.

Another way in which your space is invaded is when you are sitting at your desk. This is done by someone who comes into your office or your work area and either hovers over you or sits on your desk. You deal with this by standing up — don't just pop up like a jack-in-the-box, wait a few seconds and then have a reason to move, for example to get something out of a filing cabinet or a piece of paper off a shelf behind you. This then puts you higher than the other person and you are in the position of power.

Time control

Your timing for arrival at meetings can give an indication of your power. Powerless people usually arrive very early for meetings and wait for the more powerful to arrive. Overpowering people have a habit of arriving very late without even a good reason. The powerful person again hits the happy medium by arriving as close to the actual time as possible within a ten to fifteen minute window around the exact time. No more than ten minutes early (otherwise you have not got enough to do to keep you busy!), and no more than five minutes late — but if you are late, even if this is a power play, you must have a very good reason to give.

Silence

This is a technique often used by overpowering people, during a conversation they will leave long silences. The tendency is for you to fill that silence and take responsibility for the conversation. Do not do this, it will encourage you to say more than you want, which is exactly their purpose. There are two ways you can handle this if somebody uses the technique on you, one is to be silent yourself and wait for the other person to break the silence, the other is to ask a question which changes the topic or restarts the conversation and throws the onus back onto them.

You may like to use the technique of silence yourself: it is a way or encouraging other people to talk and is usually effective if they do not know how to handle it. Powerful people are not afraid of leaving silences in conversations, whereas the powerless tend always to want to fill them.

The hand shake

It is a ritual which we all go through when we are introduced to new people and we should do it to both male and female colleagues. But the way you give your handshake can say something about you — a limp weak handshake is powerless and a bone-crushing over-pumping handshake is overpowering. A powerful handshake should be given firmly with a warm dry hand and be given with the whole hand not just the fingers.

When two men meet for the first time it is normal for the more powerful to offer his hand first and take his hand away first. As women we are often tempted to thrust our hand forward first as soon as we are introduced to someone, almost as if it is a defence mechanism, and when the recipient is obviously more senior this can seem as if you are taking his or her power play. In this situation you want to initiate the handshake but let the other person actually do it first: one way to do this is to walk up to him, but not stand too close, and look expectantly at him without saying anything — if this doesn't work after a couple of seconds then you can glance at his hand. This usually works, but only then if you are desperate should you offer your hand first.

Looking powerful

It helps if you are tall, and therefore look imposing, but even if you are not you should 'walk tall', i.e. as if you are confident and know what you are doing. If you give an impressive of confidence others will have confidence in you.

Dress is another important aspect of being powerful. Remember that at meetings and presentations others will see you before they hear you and the way you dress will give that all important first impression. If you look like a housewife who has just come out for the day you will be treated in that way.

Your 'territory'

The accepted trappings of power (a large office, large car, big staff and budget, etc.) are territorial. Traditionally women are not empire-builders and so do not normally seek these. Unfortunately the reward system in most large companies is related to this empire-building situation and that is one of the reasons why women frequently lose out.

Your office can communicate a lot about you. Even if you do not have your own office, you will have a desk and some personal area and you can treat this as if it is your office. Although you may not be able to choose your own furnishings, you may be able to choose the way you use your space and 'accessorize' it. But the most powerful people have their own offices, even senior secretaries in large companies have their own office, so wherever possible try to get an office of your own, although this will not always be possible, especially in these days of open plan offices. Once you have got one, do not give up your office or volunteer to share it.

Do not make your office look too homely. Too many plants, too many pictures, a fluffy rug and so on, gives the impression that you 'live' here and are intending to stay and so raises the question, 'Are you not going to move up?' Your office should be clean and tidy and professional looking, and not over-fussy.

Playing the political game of power

Playing the political game is not natural to women. Women are much more straightforward, less territorial and seeking co-operation rather than conflict. Women need a comfortable working relationship and therefore won't antagonize. They are less single-minded in seeking to achieve their goals and are more likely to be masters in the 'art of the possible'.

But that does not mean that you cannot play the political game. Women have a lack of political awareness and do not take to the games of politics within companies easily. Generally they are less willing to see themselves succeed at the expense of others; this is not a bad trait but sometimes can mean that you miss opportunities.

Men are less willing to express their lack of confidence in their ability, they will not admit that they do not know something but will either bluff their way through or go and find out about it. Most women have the ability but do not sell themselves well and, through lack of confidence, do not show their ability. This is where they can learn from their male colleagues. Tell people, especially the boss, what you have achieved, volunteer to give presentations or represent your department or company on important committees. Be visible and be seen doing well.

Because women have only seen the abuse of power in the past they may shy away from it. But the old-style political and power games are not the only way: Geraldine Bown believes that we have an inner power that we can use. Women have a way of doing things differently and therefore should use this source of energy which is unique to women, we should tap into our personal power and employ it to our advantage.

In all large organizations political games are played and you need to be aware of the games, whether you choose to play or not. Women prefer a situation of co-operation in place of competition, and are uncomfortable with the win/lose situation, even being as frightened of winning as losing, because our natural care for others will identify with the problems of the loser! We are more comfortable with a win/win situation but this is not always possible in companies, and perhaps for this to change there needs to be more women in senior positions — until then we must learn to play the games by the existing rules.

The acquisition of power can depend on being aware of what the important issues are to your organization. You need to be in the departments and jobs which deal with these strategic issues and have the skills necessary to make the most of any political opportunity.

In most organizations there are issues which are especially significant for the survival and development of that organization, and these usually involve powerful groups outside the company. These issues might include things like the relationship with a major customer or some dispute with a trade union. If you are in a position to deal effectively with such issues this can enhance your power. The more exclusively you have this ability the more powerful you become (provided that the ability and its exclusiveness are recognized).

The trouble is, of course, that strategically important issues change over time and it isn't easy to have enough flexibility to change with them. Sometimes the 'luck' of being in the right place at the right time can help your acquisition of power, but in those situations unless you grab the opportunity and make use of it, it will not enhance your position. If you are not in a position where your job is directly related to the strategically important issues, it may be that you will have to persuade the powerful that your job and skills *are* still strategically important to the organization. Doing your job well is not sufficient, you must be visible and be seen to be doing an 'important' job. Combining hard work with enhancing your image and making the right contacts is the route towards this.

We must learn to look at all the options and make choices. If we take risks it can be to our advantage so long as we do it in a calculated way. Look at all the pros and cons, weigh up all the options, and say to yourself, 'What is the worst thing that can possibly happen?'. If you can cope with the worst that can happen then it is not too great a risk. If you can't cope — how can you minimize the likelihood of the worst happening?

We are all in the position of being able to make choices, even if the choice is to leave the job. In fact there is a right time for leaving a job and moving on. Programme yourself to think positively — think in terms of 'If I leave this job I can always get another one and it will be a better one', then you are in the right frame of mind for improving your career as you move. There is a time to move and change your job, and that is one of the options that you have. Don't feel trapped, have a positive attitude towards a move.

It is worthwhile spending time reading biographies and articles about important and powerful people, men as well as women, and finding out as much as possible about how they have acquired their power.

A quote from Christina Gearing: 'Whether they believe it or not, women have the real power'.

Chapter Eight

Learning the Rules and Playing the Political Game

Networking

Your personal support system can help to increase your feeling of power. Networking is an important aspect of this support system. It has been shown that you can need as many as thirty or more people in your personal network to support you. Different people will provide different types of support, including social and emotional support as well as at work. You need a variety of people in this support network, including people of both sexes.

You also need role models: good role models whom you can look up to as good examples of what you can and will achieve. Choose powerful role models who will give you the right examples and approaches that you need. One of the problems for women in very senior positions is that they have few peers and even fewer above them whom they can use as role models.

Women do not have the established network and grapevine at work in the way that men do, neither do they have the network of men's clubs. Therefore it is important that you build your own network. Women build and value their friendships and that can be a great strength — it is important to be able to talk to other women and share your experiences, not necessarily at work, but also socially. However, it is not usually wise to be too friendly or open on a personal level with your subordinates, so find women outside your company with whom you can share experience and from whom you can gain support. Even then it is not sensible to be too open and honest to anyone and you should make sure you know your listener before you pour your heart out.

Women tend to see the social side of work as a waste of time, but it may well be an essential part of the job. Many women handicap themselves because they underestimate the importance of making a wide range of business contacts. You should put yourself forward for training courses and attend conferences and seminars. It is a way of meeting people away from the workplace and of building up contacts.

When Janet Rubin was looking for a career move she was a member of the Institute of Personnel Management and on the committee of their Central London Group at that time. It was through a chance conversation with a head hunter met through the committee that she found out that Burtons were looking for someone in personnel: she was ultimately offered the job as the head of Personnel and Training for their 'Principles' Women's Wear division. Janet believes that networking is important, it is worthwhile joining groups and getting on committees and she does believe that it is through networking and talking to the right people that she has got herself noticed and been offered her positions.

Networking is important both for your career and for keeping a balance in your life in general. Everyone should have a social life and learn to switch off and recharge one's batteries.

There are a growing number of organizations which provide women with their own version of the old boy network. One problem is that a lot of women have got commitments after work and don't socialize with their colleagues as the men do. Joining clubs and social organizations gives you a way of meeting people and finding out what is going on elsewhere, for example levels of salaries and promotion, as well as giving you some social activities. In addition, talking informally to work colleagues keeps you in touch with what is happening in *your* organization. Janet Rubin says that it is also important to develop mentors and supporters; and be prepared to mix with your colleagues, for example in the bar after dinner, and be seen to do so. You must learn to be aware of political behaviour and how to deal with it.

To make the best of networking you need to understand how the informal structures operate behind the formal organization chart. You must be aware of office politics and how to play them and you can only do that by watching, listening, and learning.

The support which your network can offer is an important aid to women in the competitive environment of today. Other advantages of networking are:

- It enables you to widen the scope of your job.
- It raises your awareness of your contribution to your role.
- It widens your contacts.
- It provides background information to help you do your job more successfully.
- Sometimes it can open doors and enable you to get things done more quickly, easily and less officiously.
- It can assist in making friends and business contacts.

Professional organizations and support groups can provide the backup which is often missing within your own organization, and some of these groups are listed within the appendix at the end of the book.

You and the hierarchy

Men intuitively play the political game, probably because of the more competitive environment in which they are brought up. Women need to be alerted to the politics and learn the techniques, otherwise they may naïvely believe they are going to get on in a company just by doing a good job.

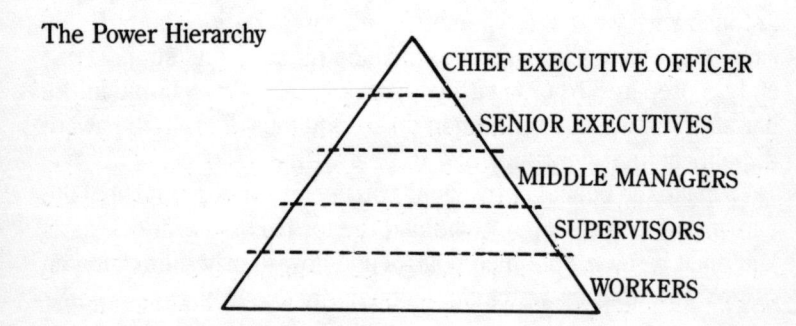

The Power Hierarchy

CHIEF EXECUTIVE OFFICER
SENIOR EXECUTIVES
MIDDLE MANAGERS
SUPERVISORS
WORKERS

It is important that you find out what the hierarchy in your organization is and where you fit into it. Traditionally, women have been less interested in this than men, but it is important to your male colleagues that they know what the hierarchy is and where they fit into it, therefore it must be important to you. Your present position is your starting point for moving up.

Where are you in this structure? Where do you want to go in the structure? And how are you going to get there?

Until you find out where you are in the hierarchy and how the hierarchy works, and decide where you want to go, you will not be in a position to move your way up.

Having decided where you are, you should remember your position in the hierarchy, especially when you are concerned about things you see and wish to change. Major changes can only be made by people in middle management positions and upwards — most organizations do not expect people below those levels to think for themselves! This is not true of all organizations, but is still true in most. If you are aspiring to management positions but spend all your time telling senior managers that they are wrong in the way they are doing things you are most likely to find that they see you as threatening.

If you are unhappy about the way things are done there are three ways of handling it: ignore it; work round it, continuing to play the game by the rules, while working your way up to a position where you are senior enough to actually do something about it; or get out. This may seem glib, but it is the way the game is played in many organizations. There may be an occasion when your ideas are genuinely sought and welcome, you must learn when this is so. Whatever you do — don't test the water by embarrassing your boss.

One of the problems for women in the past has been that traditionally most people who move into senior positions move from 'line' jobs, not from staff jobs, where women have usually been employed. Staff positions are support positions, like personnel, training and finance. Line jobs are those which are directly related to the product or service which the company offers, such as working on the production line or managing the people who work on the line or providing a direct service to the customers.

These jobs involve the 'operations' people, the people who actually get the job done. And the people who get to the top have usually been operations people, i.e. those who have had direct experience in providing the service or producing the product which is the reason for the company. So, in your career planning you should look at all the options open to you and wherever possible move into the line or operations jobs because these are the quickest routes to the top.

You can also learn by looking at those around you. Look at the people above you in the positions of power and see what type of characters they are. There will be some people within the organization who have some power because of their position, but when you look closely into it do not have any real power. In most hierarchies the individual will be the understudy for his or her boss. If the boss has no power, then nor will the subordinates. If you are planning a strategic career move, move to work for someone who has *real* power. A good boss will develop good members of his or her team and help them to move up too.

Networking is part of the hierarchical structure. Within organizations there will be two types of network, formal and informal; the larger the organization the more informal networks there will be. If you are working just through the formal networks the chances are that you are only getting your information from your boss: that should not be the only source of your information. Tap into other networks, people lateral to you, other people senior to you, and even subordinates who often find out what is happening before the boss. Networking is a very powerful communication device. It is important that you belong to a number of informal networks, this is how you keep yourself informed and ahead of the game. Information is power. But the way you use and see that information is also critical; remember that the information you receive through the informal networks will have a degree of truth, but should also be viewed with a certain amount of caution — it should also be treated as confidential. Collect and store the information to be used at an appropriate time, but be careful with whom you discuss the information; you can never be sure who plays golf with whom or who knows somebody else's brother, wife, son, mother etc . . . so be careful!

Hierarchy and skills

Where you are on the hierarchy will determine what level of skills you need and use in your job. At the lowest levels of the hierarchy you will use your technical skills; as you move up into management positions the human or interpersonal skills such as communication skills and dealing with people become more important; finally at the highest levels conceptual skills are the most important ones. So as you go higher up through the hierarchy you get less and less involved with actually doing the job you started out with. The old adage, 'if you want a job well done do it yourself', no longer applies. Your skill at the top levels is in getting other people to do the job well. This can cause us problems in two ways, firstly we are having to learn and develop new skills and techniques as we go up the hierarchy, secondly as women it is less natural for us to delegate things to other people. We are much more used to doing the job ourselves rather than asking somebody else to do it, this is part of the basic 'female' training which we have to unlearn to enable us to climb the ladder of success.

As organizations slim down to become leaner and fitter one of the things that is happening is that some of the middle management roles are being done away with. This is making it increasingly difficult to follow the logical upward steps that one might have done in the past, especially for women to whom few avenues are open anyway. In this situation there are two options. One is not to move at all, another is to move sideways. In fact lateral moves are a good option. They increase your knowledge of the company, they give you contacts with more people and they increase your skills and experience. This broader education and knowledge of the company will improve your marketability.

Managers and responsibility

There are many people that are in positions called 'manager' but are not actually managing anyone. Until you really have responsibility for other people you are not a real part of the power club.

Having a management position where you control other people means that not only do you decide what work they do and give them guidance and direction, but also you have responsibility for hiring and firing, performance appraisal and what they earn. When you reach that position you are a real member of the management club and it is at this point that life gets tough. You have to make decisions and solve problems on your own and the job is less well defined. It gets even more difficult when you are a manager over other managers. Lower level managers are supervisors who have control over people who do not themselves have any management responsibility, but middle managers have control over people of management level.

You and your boss

Remember that your prospects for promotion depend upon your boss. In choosing who to promote your boss will not only be looking for someone who has the qualifications to carry out the work, with the technical ability to do the job, but also someone with whom he or she can work. If you are someone that they find fun and enjoyable to be with then you may find that that will help you. That does not mean someone who spends all their day telling *risqué* jokes to the boss, but someone with whom the boss feels comfortable and someone whose company he or she enjoys. People are not chosen for promotion if they make other people (particularly those above them) uncomfortable. Beware of appearing to be too powerful, this makes people above you feel uncomfortable.

Performance appraisals

Critical assessment is important to you to help you improve your performance. Research has shown that when both men and women report to a male boss the male colleagues receive more constructive criticism in their appraisals than the women. Male bosses seem to have a reluctance to criticize women, particularly in a manner that will improve their performance. On being questioned as to why this was the case it seemed that male bosses are worried about how women will react to criticism. If the recipient becomes emotional, they don't know how to cope with it. An over-emotional reaction to criticism, such as crying, upsets male colleagues on two counts. Firstly, men have been brought up to expect that they will protect the women in their lives. So if a female colleague cries when she is criticized he feels that he has failed, and this will lead him to avoid criticism in the future. Also, if a woman cries when given criticism it will lead her male colleagues to believe that she cannot handle pressure and cannot cope with responsibility.

Steps to the top

People who are successful attribute their success to a number of factors, but the three main ones are hard work (10 per cent); image (30 per cent); and contacts (60 per cent). This bears out the truth in the old saying, 'It's not what you know, but who you know'. However, each one of these attributes is important and none should be completely ignored. On the question of contacts, it is not only contacts upwards but contacts with people in all directions which can help you through the knowledge that they bring as well as the advantages of their position.

Taking the steps to the top

These are the characteristics of the powerful as shown by a Harvard Business School survey some years ago. These are the keys to the top, some are behavioural, some are pure skills, but to get to the top you need to work within this system.

- Look the part and dress the part.
- Maintain self-control.
- Have perception as a team player (i.e. be *seen* as a team player): *Think boss, talk team.*

- Find powerful patrons.
- When there is a need for decision making:
  (a) do it when necessary;
  (b) do it using participative management so that the solutions can be shared.
- Have executive style. Components of executive style are:
  (a) being fast on your feet, thinking on your feet, and reacting quickly.
  (b) giving slick presentations, being able to step in at a moment's notice and give a slick, good presentation. Stand up in front of a group and present yourself well, ad-libbing as necessary.
  (c) appearing knowledgeable, using correct terms and jargon, etc.
  (d) subtle sophistication, witty, smooth, behaviour. This includes clothes, carriage, the way you deal with people, and communication skills.

Political knowhow

As well as these steps there are the unwritten rules of political knowhow. These are:

- Do realize that the boss *is* the boss.
- Do keep the boss informed.
- Do make the boss look good.
- Do work towards getting the boss promoted.
- Do not commit the sin of going over your boss' head to his boss.
- Do not talk disparagingly about your company or colleagues in public.
- Do not destroy those who oppose you, allow them to save face.
- Do not overlook the importance of social events.

Women and success

If women want to get to the top there are some aspects about themselves they may need to change and some disadvantages to overcome but also some strengths to be capitalized on. It was never easy for men to achieve success in business but unlike women they are assumed to be competent until they are proved incompetent. Women do have difficulties and problems over and above those of their male colleagues but they also have a number of advantages. Senior women are still unusual and can capitalize on this. Clare Gallagher benefited from this: because she is unusual in her position she got noticed and remembered. Clare was recommended for the Business Woman of the Year award by the then Chairman of ICI, John Harvey Jones, who had only met her on one or two occasions but remembered her.

You cannot do everything and will have to let some things go to meet the demands of a career. Men expect women employees to give them the same loyalty that their wives give them and they expect more from women, feeling more hurt when women let them down or leave. You may have to make some mistakes to learn but treat each one as a learning experience.

Objectives and goals

Although we do not see ourselves this way many women are innovators and want a challenge. When their objectives have been achieved they are not happy to coast along and want to move on to something new. Women's ability to cope with many different things and manage crisis is part of the explanation of this trend. Although we will have a routine and a way of organizing things, women are not creatures of habit in the way that men are, and are thus more able to cope with change and challenge than many of their male colleagues. This was an obvious trait in all the women I met while researching this book.

When women are set an objective, or set themselves an objective, they see that objective ahead and work towards it; a woman will quietly make her mind up to do something and then get on and do it. (Although some men are capable of doing this, especially the directive types, they may worry more about the route to that objective and not get on so quickly and decisively with the job in hand.) This is a broad generalization and is truer of women who are achievers than of those who are content to stay in more mundane and less challenging tasks.

Women are also frequently self-critical, this is fine so long as it is constructive, and not destructive. Think about what you have done and how you have performed, look at how you can improve it and learn from each experience.

We are also very tenacious. If you believe in what you are doing — don't give up, eventually you will persuade others to come with you.

Remember that success is 80 per cent attitude and only 20 per cent skills and knowledge. Promote and position yourself for power but also remember that personal power is *with* people not *over* people.

You can do it

Look back at Chapter 2 and the goals you made then. Do you want to add to these in the light of what you have read and learnt? If so then do it now.

Before you move on you need to decide what you want, then you can work on how to get there. The first step is to find out what is important to you.

Look at the list below and rank the points in order of importance to you. Put one against the factor that is most important, two against the next and so on.

- **A.** Advancement and opportunities for promotion (M).
- **B.** Interesting work (M).
- **C.** Job possibilities for individual growth (M).
- **D.** Job security (H).
- **E.** Personal relationships with superiors (H).
- **F.** Personal relationships with colleagues (H).

G. Personal relationships with subordinates (H).
H. Recognition for effective work (M).
I. Responsibility (for example finance or people) (M).
J. Satisfaction in the job (M).
K. Salary (H).
L. Working conditions (physical) (H).

Some of the factors listed here are called motivators and some are hygiene factors; this means that the motivators (M) are those which will motivate and encourage you while the hygiene factors (H) are those which are nice to have but not essential to you. If you find that in ranking the list the (M)s are higher than the (H)s then you are motivated by success and achievement; if the (H)s are higher than the (M)s then you are likely to need comfort and security more than success. Is this a true reflection of your needs? To get on you must *want* to get on.

Making an action plan

So what is your next move? Make an action plan and work to it. Writing down what you will do is the first stage in your commitment and will make you begin.

Action plan

What do I want?

What am I worth?

When do I want to reach this?

How can I help my boss/company to justify this salary?

Do my salary homework. Find out what others in my field are making and see if my current salary is in line. Make sure the people who count know what I have contributed.

Revamp my wardrobe and invest in myself.	*(Make a separate list of things you will do in this context and the dates by which you will do them.)*

Keep visible. Make a list of ways I can be seen to be doing a good job and by whom. Remember tricks like writing updates on my projects to important people.

Let people know I want promotion.	*(Don't overdo this but make sure that you are told of any opportunities available and that you are looked at for promotion.)*
I will succeed by doing................	
I will help my team by doing.....	*(Help your team to succeed. The quickest way to get ahead is by having a team of good people around you, don't hold them back; help them.)*
I will use and build the skills I have:	*(Look back at your skills list from Chapter 2 and list them here.)*
I will work on the skills I need:	*(Set a date by when you will have worked on each skill and how you will achieve this; e.g. go on a course or get in-house training. Tick off each skill as you acquire it — make sure you really have got it !)*

NOW GO AND PUT YOUR PLAN INTO ACTION!!

Appendix
Useful Names
and Addresses

Academic Women's Achievement Group
Professor Hannah Steinberg
Convenor
Academic Women's Achievement Group
University College London
Gower Street
London WC1E 6BT   Tel: 071 387 7050 & 071 380 7232

Association of Personal Assistants & Secretaries
Ms Isobel Brown McPhail
Chairman
Association of Personal Assistants & Secretaries
14 Victoria Terrace
Royal Leamington Spa
Warwickshire   Tel: 0926 24844/24794

Association of Women in Public Relations
Ms Janet Hildreth
Association of Women in Public Relations
27 Great James Street
London WC1N 3ES

Association of Women Solicitors
Ms Patricia Cunningham
Association of Women Solicitors
The Law Society
8 Bream's Buildings
London EC4A 1HP   Tel: 071 404 4355

British Association of Women Entrepreneurs
Ms Nora Liddle Terek
British Association of Women Entrepreneurs
303 Preston Road
Harrow
Middlesex   Tel: 081 904 1412

British Women Pilots' Association
Ms Lola McRobert
Hon. Secretary
British Women Pilots' Association
Rochester Airport
Chatham
Kent ME5 9SD

Businesswoman's Travel Club
A non-profit making organization which aims to improve services for the travelling businesswoman. They maintain a database of hotels worldwide that welcome, and cater especially for, businesswomen. They will also supply information from surveys they have conducted and have a newsletter which gives useful advice. Information from:

Businesswoman's Travel Club Ltd
10 Strutton Ground
London SW1P 2HP   Tel: 071 222 4539

Centre for Research on European Women
Centre for Research on European Women
38 Rue Stevin
1040 Brussels
Belgium

Commonwealth Secretariat,
Women & Development Programme
Commonwealth Secretariat, Women & Development Programme
Marlborough House
Pall Mall
London SW1Y 5HX   Tel: 071 839 3411

Appendix — Useful names and addresses

Equal Opportunities Commission
Overseas House
Quay Street
Manchester M3 3HN   Tel: 061 833 9244

European Association of Professional Secretaries
Mrs M. Lathia
European Association of Professional Secretaries
c/o Sir Bruce White, Barry & Partners
Douglas House
Douglas Street
London SW1P 4PB

European Union of Women
Mrs M.A. Barkes JP
European Union of Women
32 Smith Square
London SW1P 3HH   Tel: 071 222 9000

European Women's Management Development Network
European Women's Management Development Network
Rue Washington 40
B-1050 Brussels
Belgium   Tel: (02) 648 03 85

European Women's Management Development Network (UK)
c/o Ms Valerie Hammond
Director of Research
Ashridge Management College
Berkhamsted
Herts HP4 1NS   Tel: 044 284 3491

Fawcett Society
Fawcett Society
46 Harleyford Road
London SE11 5AY   Tel: 071 587 1287

Federation of Business & Professional Women
Federation of Business & Professional Women
23 Ansdell Street
London W8 5BN   Tel: 071 938 1729

FOCUS
FOCUS Information Service
47/49 Gower Street
London WC1E 6HR

Institute of Qualified Private Secretaries
Miss R. Betts
Institute of Qualified Private Secretaries
126 Farnham Road
Slough SL1 4XA   Tel: 0753 22395

Medical Women's Federation
Mrs V. Lenton
Executive Secretary
Medical Women's Federation
Tavistock House North
Tavistock Square
London WC1H 9HX   Tel: 071 387 7765

National Advisory Centre on Careers For Women
Mrs J. Hurley
National Advisory Centre on Careers for Women
8th Floor
Artillery House
Artillery Row
London SW1P 1RT   Tel: 071 799 2129

National Association of Women Pharmacists
National Association of Women Pharmacists
Pharmaceutical Society of Great Britain
1 Lambeth High Street
London SE1 7JN   Tel: 071 707 0796

National Council of Women
Mrs J.D. Norman
National Council of Women
36 Danbury Street
Islington
London N1 8JN   Tel: 071 354 2395

National Joint Committee of Working Women's Organizations
National Joint Committee of Working Women's Organizations
150 Walworth Road
London SE17 1JT

National Organization for Women's Management Education
Ms Yvonne Sarch
National Organization for Women's Management Education
12a Westbere Road
London NW2 3RR   Tel: 071 794 8734

Network
An organization which sets up meetings about issues of interest to women and gives an opportunity to meet other women with career interests. Meetings national and some local groups.

Network
25 Park Road
London NW1 6XN   Tel: 071 402 1285

The Peperell Unit
The Industrial Society
48 Bryanston Square
London W1H 7LN   Tel: 071 839 4300

Rights of Women Europe Group
Ms Vanessa Hall Smith
Rights of Women Europe Group
10 Tredegar Road
London E3   Tel: 081 980 4308

Soroptimist International
Soroptimist International of Great Britain & Ireland
63 Bayswater Road
London W2 3PJ   Tel: 071 262 4794

300 Group
Ms Elaine Hendry
Administrator
300 Group
9 Poland Street
London W1V 3DG   Tel: 071 734 3457

Wardrobe
You can obtain advice on dressing and presenting yourself, as well as clothes, at this shop.

Ms S. Faux
'Wardrobe'
3 Grosvenor Street
London W1

Women and Training Group
Women & Training Group,
Hewmar House
120 London Road
Gloucester GL1 3TL   Tel: 0452 309330

Women & Manual Trades
Women & Manual Trades
52-54 Featherstone Street
London EC1   Tel: 071 251 9192/3

Women in Banking
Ms Deborah Simon
Women in Banking
Target Life Assurance
Alton House
174/177 High Holborn
London WC1

Women in Civil Service
Ms Rita O'Brien
Women in Civil Service
Department of Industry
Ashdown House
123 Victoria Street
London SW1

Women in Computing
Women in Computing
c/o Micro Sister
Wesley House
4 Wild Court
London WC2   Tel: 071 430 0655

Women in Construction Advisory Group
Women in Construction Advisory Group
Room 182 Southbank House
Black Prince Road
London SE1 7SJ   Tel: 071 587 8171/0028/1507/1802

Women in Enterprise
Women in Enterprise
26 Bond Street
Wakefield WF1 2QP   Tel: 0924 361789

Women in Industry
Ms Kirsty Ross
Women in Industry
Red Gables
130 Brighton Road
Hooley
Coulsdon
Surrey CR2 3EF

Women in Management
Ms Elizabeth Harman
Executive Secretary
Women in Management
64 Marryat Road
Wimbledon
London SW19 5BN   Tel: 081 946 1238

Women in Medicine
Ms V.J. Holt
Women in Medicine
7c Cassland Road
London E9   Tel: 081 986 1275

Women in Printing Trades Group
c/o Ms Lucy Boughton
28 Salton Road
London SW2 1EP   Tel: 071 274 6091

Women in Publishing
Membership Secretary
Women in Publishing
c/o 12 Dyott Street
London WC1A 1DF

Women in Telecom
c/o Ms Denise Maguire
STE Office
Room 212/13 Bath House
52 Holborn Viaduct
London EC1A 2ET   Tel: 071 936 3197

Women into Business:
A group established by the small business bureau to encourage more women to consider business ownership and to provide support for women already in business. Membership details from:

Women into Business
Small Business Bureau
32 Smith Square
London SW1P 3HH   Tel: 071 222 0330

Women Returners' Network
Women Returners' Network
Ms Ann Bell
Principal
Chelmsford Adult Education Centres
Patching Hall Lane
Chelmsford
Essex CM1 4DB   Tel: 0245 358631

Women's Advertising Club of London
Women's Advertising Club of London
Ms Ros Todd
Donavon Data Systems
Berger House
7 Farm Street
London W1X 7RB					Tel: 071 629 7654

Women's Computer Centre
Women's Computer Centre
Wesley House
4 Wild Court
London WC28 5AU					Tel: 071 430 0112

Women's Engineering Society
Women's Engineering Society
Imperial College of Science & Technology
Department of Civil Engineering
Imperial College Road
London SW7 2BU					Tel: 071 589 5111

Women's Enterprise Development Agency
Ms Elaine Lawrence
Women's Enterprise Development Agency
Aston Science Park
Love Lane
Aston Triangle
Birmingham B7 4BJ					Tel: 021 359 0178

Women's Film Television & Video Network
Women's Film Television & Video Network
79 Wardour Street
London W1V 3PH					Tel: 071 434 2076

Women Motor Mechanics Workshop Ltd
Women's Motor Mechanics Workshop Ltd
Bay 4R
1-3 Brixton Road
London SW9 6DE					Tel: 071 582 2574

Women's National Commission
Women's National Commission
Government Offices
Great George Street
London SW1P 2AQ   Tel: 071 270 3000

Women's Travel Club of Great Britain
Women's Travel Club of Great Britain
Ms Jane Wilton
Atlantida Travel
21 Garrick Street
London WC2E 9AZ

Working Mothers Association
Working Mothers Association
7 Spenser Walk
London SW15 1PL   Tel: 081 788 2565

Working Women's Organization
Working Women's Organization
c/o Ms Linda Kirkbride
20 Summerhill Road
Cowplain
Portsmouth PO8 8XE   Tel: 0705 263776

Zonta International
Ms Sheila Marshall
Area Director UK
Zonta International
20 Upland Park Road
Oxford OX2 7RU   Tel: 0865 56936

Training materials etc

Business Women's Training Institute
Runs seminars for training women in key management skills. Information from:

Business Women's Training Institute
793 Weston Road
Slough
Berkshire SL1 4HP   Tel: 0753 820277

Domino Training Ltd
An independent training company which produces packs for self study and for use with groups, including 'Women into Management'.

Domino Training
56 Charnwood Road
Shepshed
Leicestershire LE12 9NP   Tel: 0509 505404

Open University
The OU Business School runs a course called 'Women into Management'. Details from:

The Open University
Walton Hall
Milton Keynes MK7 6AA   Tel: 0908 652412

'Women in Partnership' Video
Details and loan from:

Commission of the European Communities
8 Storey's Gate
London SW1 3AT   Tel: 071 222 8122

Contact the **Women & Training Group** for a list of the training materials which they produce or know of, many free.

Women & Training Group
Hewmar House
120 London Road
Gloucester GL1 3TL   Tel: 0452 309330

Index

accommodating behaviour 97
accounting 116, 117
action plans 173-4
aggressive behaviour 63-4, 86, 145-6
'agreeable' people, dealing with 95
analyst-type people 87-8, 89, 92-4
anger 103
annual report and accounts 117
assertive behaviour 85-6, 145-6, 151-2
assertiveness skills 146-51
   training 62, 151, 152
attitudes, changing 55-6
auditory-type people 79-80
authority, formal 153, 154

balance sheet 118, 119
battles, fighting 97-9
being heard 81-3, 98
body language 45-6, 79, 84, 86, 107
bosses
   harrassment from 68
   relationship with 65-6, 83, 168, 170
   see also hierarchies
Bown, Geraldine 14, 36, 60, 62, 63, 105, 106, 160
British Institute of Management 8
business jargon 120-1

career planning 17, 28-32, 166
case studies 11-22
cash flow 120
cash management 119-20

change, coping with 171
charisma 152
childhood experiences 37, 38, 53-4
choices 33, 161
Clarke, Liz 9, 12-13, 62, 111, 139, 151
clothes 48-51
colours 50
communication skills 42-7, 77-83, 81-3, 107, 125
   barriers to 43–4
   see also verbal communication; written communication
complaints, dealing with 92-3
computing jargon 121-4
conditioning 41, 53-4, 56-7, 60
contacts 163, 169
   see also networking
contributions, making 59-60
control 152, 168
   dealing with loss of 96
   see also power; self-control
coping 108, 171
cost accounting 117
criticism 37-8
   dealing with 68-71, 128, 168-9
   self- 172
crying 58-9, 169

decision-making 109, 111-14, 170
delegation 109, 110-11, 117
diet 101-2
difficult people, dealing with 83-97
   identifying types 86-8

directive-type people 87, 88, 89, 90-2
disciplining staff 143-4
Dixson, Anne 17-18, 72, 107, 110
dress 48-51, 79, 158, 169

eating out 41-2
effectiveness 108
efficiency 108
emotions 57–9, 103
  expressing 58, 107, 146, 169
employment
  personal history *see* work history
  statistics 7-8
  trends 7-8
Employment Protection
  (Consolidation) Act (1978) 67
enjoyment 40
executive style 170
  see also management style
exercise 101-2
experience
  assessing 24-6, 41
  learning from 12, 17, 33, 41, 42, 102, 171
expressive-type people 87, 88, 89, 95-6
eye contact 45

facial expression 44-5
family matters 59
family structures 53
Faux, Susie 13, 48, 49, 50
feedback 82-3, 85, 130
feelings *see* emotions
financial data 116-20
financial jargon 115-16
financial position 116
flexibility 96-7
fogging 149

Gallagher, Clare 18-19, 61, 72, 76, 105, 171
Gearing, Christina 14-16, 41, 59, 140, 161
getting your message across 126, 127-8, 150-1
goals
  achieving 171-2
  career 17, 28-30, 171-2

  personal 36-7
  setting 17, 28-30, 172-4

handshakes 158
health 101-2
hierarchies 164-7
honesty 58
humour, sense of 98
Hunt, Margaret 16-17, 64, 66

image 35, 169
influence 153, 154, 155
information 109, 114, 166
  gathering 113
  giving and withholding 81-3, 114
interpersonal skills 143-4, 146, 153
interruptions, dealing with 90-1, 128, 150-1
investors 116

jargon 114-24
job satisfaction 26

kinesthetic-type people 79-80
know-it-all, dealing with a 96
knowledge 109, 114, 153
  see also information

labour force 7-8
language 114-24
learned behaviour 39
  see also conditioning
letters, writing 132-3, 135
line jobs 165
listening 81, 106

make-up 50
management style
  Japanese 127
  men 54-5, 160
  women 74-5, 125, 127, 143-4
marriage 11
media 43
meetings 124-30
  group 126-9
  holding 129-30
  one-to-one 126
memos, writing 132-5

Index

men 52-6
　attitudes to women 55-61
　dealing with 63-4
　management style 64-5, 160
　women as threats to 56, 73
　working for women 65
　see also sensual remarks; sex differences; sexism
moving with the job 72

negative enquiry technique 149
negative feedback 36, 37
negative feelings 36, 38-9, 103
negative thinkers, dealing with 93-4
networking 71-2, 162-4, 166
non-verbal communication 44-6, 79-82, 107
note-taking 128

objectives see goals
obstacles, overcoming 32
office politics 159-74
old boys' networks 71-2, 162, 163
'operations' people 166
opportunities, taking 30-1, 154
organizational issues 160-1
organizational structures 163-6
organizing skills 109

pacing 84-5
paperwork, managing 130-8
passive behaviour 85-6, 146
people
　dealing with 33, 76-7, 83-97
　see also communication
performance appraisal 168-9
persistence 148
personal development 36-40
personal life 59
personal space 156-7
personality types 79, 81, 86-96
planning 102-3, 108, 109, 110, 129-30
　see also career planning
political games see office politics
positive affirmations 39
positive thinking 36, 37, 38, 39-40, 161
power 145-6, 152-61, 172
　appearance and 158
　games 81, 159-61

hierarchies 164-7, 170
　skills 156-61
　sources of 153-4
　web exercise 155
prejudice 56
　see also stereotyping
presentations, making 138-42
pressure, handling 99-102
problem-solving 109, 111-14
problems
　dealing with 76-7
　discussing 101
professionalism 12, 152
profit 116
profit and loss account 117, 119
project management techniques 103
promotion 72, 167, 168
public speaking 138-42
'put downs', dealing with 148-50

rapport, establishing 79-81
recreation 101-2
reflection 112
relator-type people 87, 88, 89, 94-5
relaxation 101-2
repetition 82
replaying 85
reports, writing 132-3, 135-8
requests, refusing 147-8
resources, control of 153
responsibility 167-8
rights 85-6, 145
role models 39-40, 42, 162
Rubin, Janet 19-22, 61, 72, 75, 105, 163

saying no 108
secretaries 61
self-assessment 23-8
self-control 169
self-image 35-8, 45, 52-3, 151
　improving 38-40
self-presentation 44-6
sensual remarks 61-4
sex differences 652-6, 74, 126-7, 143
Sex Discrimination Act (1975) 66, 67
sexism 61-4
sexual discrimination 66-8
sexual harrassment 63-4, 66-8

shoes 51
silence 82, 157-8
skills
  assessment 14, 24-6, 31
  hierarchies and 167
  home-based management 105-6
  key 105-9, 143-4
  see also types of skills
speaking see verbal communication
speaking out 59, 98
staff jobs 165
stalling tactics, dealing with 94
steamrollering, dealing with 91-2
steps to the top 169-70
stereotyping 56-60
strengths and weaknesses 36
stress 99-104
  assessing 99-100
  and personality types 89-96
success 171, 172
  analysing 41
  enjoying 40-1
  measures of 8, 11
  promoting 32-3

teamwork 54-5, 89, 169
  building 107
territory 159
  see also work space
thinking
  negative 36, 38-9, 93-4, 103
  positive 36, 37, 38, 39–40, 161
  productive 111-14

time
  assessing use of 23-4
  control 157
  management 102-3, 112
training 26, 143
travelling 41-2

values
  conflicts of 73-4
  and power 154-5
Van Der Salm, Anne 15, 61, 108
verbal communication 46, 77-9, 81-3,
    84-5, 107, 138-42
  barriers to 43-4
visual-type people 79-80
visualization 39
voice 44, 84

wealth 116
women
  changing roles 55-6
  expectations 52-3
  skills 105-8
  style of management 74-5, 125,
    127, 143-4
  undervaluing 60-1
  in work force 7-8
  working for women 65-6
  see also sex differences
work history 25-6, 27
work space 131, 157, 159
written communication 46, 130-8

Of further interest:

Super Confidence

The woman's guide to getting what you want out of life

Gael Lindenfield

The confident woman is someone who has mastered the skills of self-assurance, and these days, she calls the shots.

- She is fun to be with because she makes other people feel good about themselves.
- She is successful at work because she knows how to make the most of her talents.
- She uses criticism and anger constructively.
- She knows how to create fulfilling and lasting relationships.

Confident women are open, genuine and secure. They can relax because they don't feel they have to prove themselves constantly. They are achievers, too, because they are optimistic — and that lets them think creatively.

These confident women are not a breed apart. They have built up their self-assurance — and so can you. By working through the exercises in *Super Confidence* you can bring your own inner confidence to life. Then, you too can stand tall and bring out the best in your relationships and your work.

Gael Lindenfield is author of the best-selling *Assert Yourself*. She works as a freelance psychotherapist and groupwork consultant and runs courses in self-assertiveness.

Survive the Nine to Five
Every woman's guide to working well
Diana Lamplugh

Are you fit for work? Every working woman would answer this question straightaway with a definite, 'Yes, of course I am!'

But think about it. Do you take time to exercise regularly? Do you eat healthy meals based on sound nutritional guidelines? Are your desk and chair properly adjusted to allow you to sit with good posture? Do you have a positive attitude to your job and yourself to allow you to cope with the stresses and strains of everyday working life?

Survive the Nine to Five will enable you to do just that. In it you will find an exercise plan that can be fitted into the busiest working day, advice on how to eat sensibly without gaining weight, and guidance on beating stress through relaxation and attitude. There is also a discussion of some of the issues facing working women — personal safety, pregnancy at work and, most of all, how to *enjoy* your job.

Following Diana Lamplugh's advice will help you to achieve optimal physical and mental well being to allow you to give of your very best at work and to make the most of your time away from the office.